DRAGON BONES

Dragon Bones

Two Years Beneath the Skin of a Himalayan Kingdom

Murray Gunn

BLACKSMITH BOOKS

Dragon Bones

ISBN 978-988-19002-5-8

Published by Blacksmith Books
5th Floor, 24 Hollywood Road, Central, Hong Kong
Tel: (+852) 2877 7899
www.blacksmithbooks.com

Dedication

To the children of the Thunder Dragon and to Dominique, who set me on a new path.

Acknowledgements

This book exists because so many people took the time to let me experience their perspectives of life in Bhutan. Some names have been changed, but they'll all know who they are. To them, I say '*kadin che la.*'

Learning to capture the depth of a scene in words was a delightfully painful process and I'm indebted to the members of the Brussels Writers Group who guided me through countless rewrites of an earlier work until I got it right. I wouldn't have considered writing *Dragon Bones* if it hadn't been for their patience. Thanks also to George Mallory, Donna Calcandis, Derek Smith, Nisha-Anne D'Souza, Shaun Coleman, Noeline Turton and Andrew Khoo of the Friday Night Writing Group in Sydney who helped me tame this dragon.

To all my friends and family who believed in me enough to push me into taking up the challenge of writing so many years ago, thank you for believing in me.

And a special thanks to Dominique for giving me a chance so few are given.

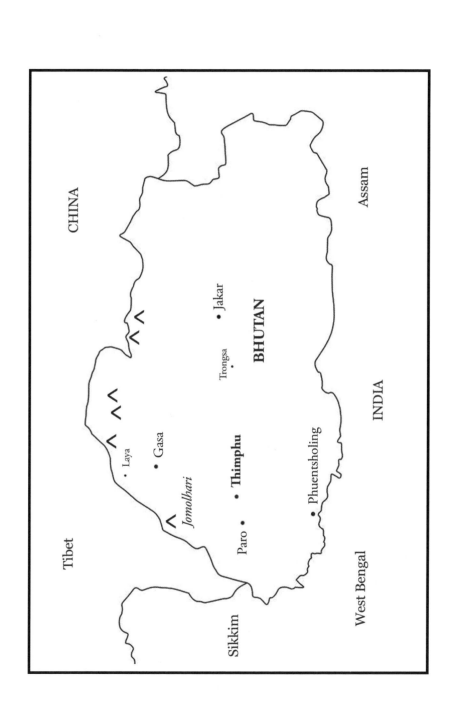

Glossary

ara	alcohol made from food grains
chilip	foreigner (mostly used for white people)
dasho	high-ranking official
datshi	cheese
dhal	Indian lentil dish
doma	betel nut chewed as a stimulant
dzong	monastic castle, these days housing government and monks
dzongkhag	political division of Bhutan
ema	chilli
gho	traditional Bhutanese garment for men
kabne	males' formal scarf to wear in dignified areas or official places
kadin che	thank you
kera	belt
kewa	potato
kira	traditional Bhutanese garment for women
kuzu zangpo	hello
la	honorific added at end of sentence
lafu	turnip
lakhang	monastery

meshu meshu	no thank you (when offered food or drink)
Nu/ngultrum	Bhutanese currency (equal to one Indian rupee)
rachu	females' formal scarf to wear in dignified areas or official places
pakora	Indian fried vegetable dish
phapsha pa	sliced pork dish
puja	religious ceremony
samosa	Indian pasty
suja	a hot drink made with salty butter
tego	upper dress traditional shirt (worn under *gho* by men or outside *kira* for women)
thukpa	Tibetan soup and dumpling dish
tsetchu	festival (tenth date of every month, an auspicious day for offerings)

Dominique's grip tightened on my hand when the Parisian Mayor paused. It signalled my turn to speak, but I suddenly realised that I didn't know the French words for 'I do.'

Three years living in Brussels and ten months of weekend visits to see Dominique in Paris hadn't been enough for me to learn her language properly. I turned my head to see her round, pretty face framed by dark hair. Her narrow brown eyes gazed adoringly at me through silver-rimmed glasses and my breath caught. She's lovely, I thought, but was I ready to change my life so significantly for this woman?

The idea of moving to live in a developing country didn't scare me. While I'd only ever lived in the first world, I'd already come a long way from my home in Australia and had been fascinated by Dominique's stories of living in Chile and Cameroon.

What little I knew about Bhutan came from a half-episode of Michael Palin's *Himalaya* and an article on Gross National Happiness, which the kingdom used in place of economic indicators. They called their country the Land of the Thunder Dragon. It sounded a wonderful country to explore.

Nor did I worry about putting my IT career on hold for a year. My company had promised me a position when I returned and I was looking forward to exploring my creative side and doing some private study.

Dominique gave me an encouraging smile which quickened my pulse and I realised my thoughts were skittering. I focused on the woman in front of me, the woman I was about to commit to forever.

That was my big fear – signing away my independence. Forever was a long time to be with a woman I'd met only last winter. When I'd caught her eye across the crowded cafeteria in the ski fields of the French Alps, I'd had no idea things would go this far. We'd talked about me joining Dominique on this assignment in Bhutan, but when the "Marry him or go alone" ultimatum came through from her employer, there hadn't been time to think.

We'd taken the French Ministry of Foreign Affairs at their word and I'd spent many sleepless nights chasing the papers required from Australia. No matter how today turned out, Dominique would board the next plane to Bhutan. I'd take a couple more weeks to tie up loose ends before following her. Or I'd go back to my old life.

The mayor shifted her weight as the pause extended. Dominique's smile changed to concern, reminding me of the gaps we still had to bridge. Eight years my junior, she was an agro-economical engineer. I didn't even understand what that was, though I knew she'd been called to help Bhutanese farmers build their dairy industry. Then there was her fiery temper, the frequent contrast to her insecurity that often left me scalded. But she was quick to smile again, quick to apologise if the anger had truly been unreasonable. Few women would do that. And she inspired me with her passion, her desire to help feed the developing world.

Marriage to Dominique would be an adventure to be tackled the same way we both attacked languages and travel. It didn't matter if we made mistakes as long as our attitudes were positive and we were ready to learn. With that thought, I knew what to say.

'Oui.'

'Are you Murray?' The slim girl who stopped me as I took my first steps onto Bhutanese soil had a round face, narrow brown eyes, olive skin and stood about shoulder height to me, but this girl wasn't Dominique. Her short black hair and traditional dress marked her clearly as a local.

'Yes, I am, but I'm sorry. Who are you?'

'I'm Selden. You'll be staying in my parents' house. Dominique's going to be another hour, so she asked me to meet you. Come and sit down.'

Her calm, assured manner left me little choice. I picked up my bags and followed her to a kiosk window. It looked out over the parking lot to the mountains just fifty metres away.

'Where's Dominique?' I asked as she ordered two teas. And more importantly, 'Why is she going to be late?'

'Actually, she's going to be on time. You're early. Your flight normally stops in Kathmandu, but because the Maoists have started causing problems again today it flew straight here.'

She picked up the tea and pointed me to a park bench in the sun. I put down my bags and removed my coat. The pilot had announced the temperature as ten degrees Celsius as we landed, but it felt hot. And the red rock and dry scrub on the surrounding slopes would look more at home in a desert than a mountain valley.

'How did you manage to get here so quickly if Dominique couldn't?'

'I work here. In the cargo section.' She pointed to the furthest building, whitewashed mud like the others, and decorated with the same arched windows and eaves of painted wood. 'The cargo won't be unloaded for another hour, so I was just playing solitaire on the computer.'

The fierce sun beat down on me until I was forced to remove my jumper. 'Is winter always this hot?'

'It snowed a couple of days ago and the plane couldn't land, but it's always warm in the sun. You'll be freezing tonight if that makes you feel better.'

I barely caught the smirk.

'So, how do you like Bhutan so far?'

I looked up at the surrounding hills across the car park. 'It's beautiful, like sloping deserts, but there isn't as much life here as I expected.' A dog barked in the distance as if to prove me wrong.

'No, there isn't much life in winter.' She stood up. 'Here they come.'

A tiny red car screeched through the parking lot, shuddering to a halt in front of us, rust flakes floating to the ground. Dominique got out of the passenger seat, looking gorgeous in a pink and brown *kira* – the traditional dress for women. Her hair, not dark enough to be black, set her apart from Selden and the other locals, but in a *kira* she could almost pass as Bhutanese.

We'd been separated for two weeks, but here I was with my wife in Bhutan, starting the adventure of a lifetime. I wanted to pick her up and spin her around. Even more, I wanted to race her home to bed.

Dominique gave me a shy smile as she walked around the car, then moved in for a quick hug. She left one hand held towards me as she stepped back as if nearly touching was the best compromise between desire and protocol.

'This is Anna,' she said, indicating the car's driver.

Anna, the woman Dominique was replacing, was in action as soon as we'd shaken hands. 'We've got to get back for lunch and then there's a lot to cover this afternoon. Bye, Selden.'

The road led out of the airport and along the valley for a short distance before climbing the sides of the hills. I reached back and felt Dominique grab my hand.

Anna chatted away in French-English while accelerating on the fifty-metre straights and slowing to swing the car around each corner. I clutched the handle above the door, glad she drove in the centre of the road as there were few barriers to stop us plummeting hundreds of metres down the steep slope to the river below. 'Are there many accidents here?' I asked as we rounded a blind corner.

A truck appeared in the middle of the road ahead and I stuck my free hand on the dashboard, bracing for either collision or fall.

'Quite a few,' said Anna, slamming on the brakes, but heading straight for the truck. Only once she'd slowed to a crawl did she turn the wheel and ease us over to the left, inches away from flying. Through wide eyes, I noticed the truck do the same, almost stopping before moving to hug the cliff. 'But if you keep your wits about you and don't try to turn while doing fifty, you'll be fine.'

'Does anyone survive a fall like that?'

'Not many. They say the only way to survive is to jump out as soon as you leave the road.' She paused. 'Of course, others say that the only way to survive is to wear your seatbelt. If something did go wrong, it'd be over before you could think about it. My plan is not to go over at all.'

Around the next blind corner, a herd of cattle strolled along in the same direction as us. I cursed as we skidded to a stop just behind the rump of a huge bull. Anna waved at the herder, tooted again and the bull ambled to one side, but there was another cow in front of that.

'They don't have any other way of moving cattle, so it's a shared road.'

From the back seat, Dominique said, 'I like it. I think it gives the place more atmosphere.'

I turned and shared a smile with her. 'We're here! We're in Bhutan at last.'

Another vehicle approached from the far side so that the herd was pressed between two cars and no amount of horn honking could clear the mess. Anna pushed into any gap that appeared and after minutes of inching along, we were suddenly free and racing off at ski jump speeds again.

'Dominique says you work in IT.'

'That's right.'

'Great. You'll be able to help her with the database then.'

I'd heard something of this. 'The one for tracking the family tree of the cattle?'

'And the milk production of each cow so that we can mate the best bulls and cows without inbreeding.'

'Yes, I got that. I usually manage conferencing services, like video-conferencing, but I thought web design might be more useful here so I've started learning a bit about databases. I might be able to help, but I don't understand why you're not using open source technologies.'

'Why would we?'

'Because developing countries would be better off not having to pay for licences.'

'Who pays for licences in Bhutan?'

'Ah. I see.'

'What about your writing?'

'That's the main reason I wanted to take the year off. I wrote a book on Japanese culture that I want to get published and I'm trying my hand at science fiction for fun.'

Ahead, the road ducked into a valley and appeared again a scant thirty metres ahead of us. I half expected Anna to try clearing the gap. Thankfully she didn't and we finally descended into a confluence of rivers, guarded by policemen in blue uniforms decorated with lanyards and epaulettes. Anna stopped to present her licence and the car's registration papers.

'Bhutan is broken up into governmental sections called *dzongkhags*,' she told me, 'and they control who crosses the borders tightly – especially foreigners.'

The policeman looked at the bags in the back. 'Coming from the airport?'

'Yes.'

One of his colleagues held two fingers up to his mouth as if smoking an imaginary cigarette and raised his eyebrows at Anna.

'Smoking's just been banned nationally,' she whispered to me before cautiously offering him her packet. 'Am I in trouble?'

'No Ma'am.' He grinned as he took one. 'Thank you Ma'am.'

Anna assured me that my bags would be safe in the car and led us into a local store for lunch. The room just inside the front door was set up like a corner store grocery with milk, biscuits, instant noodles, bottled water and whisky among other things. I followed Anna through to a back room where three of Dominique's male colleagues waited for us, all wearing *ghos* – the traditional costume for men. Made from checked material belted at the waist and hanging just below the knees, it looked like a dressing gown, but these men wore them with the dignity of Roman senators.

'With egg or without?' the one called Phuentso asked me after introductions.

'Egg with what?' I hadn't even seen a menu.

'Noodles,' Dominique said. 'It's all they serve here.'

Fair enough. Something like a *raamen* bar in Japan, then. I pictured a large bowl filled with noodles and soup, garnished with garlic, pickles, meat, and some vegetables. 'With.'

'So,' said Phuentso, who had a tall, slight build like mine. 'You're in Bhutan as Dominique's dependent.'

'I guess I am.'

'How does it feel to be a house husband?'

'House husband!' the other Bhutanese repeated, laughing and I found it easy to join in.

'I hope I'll be doing more than washing clothes and cooking.'

I leant back to let the waitress place my meal in front of me. A raw egg and a clump of chilli sauce sat beside a small bowl of packet noodles.

'This is my office,' Dominique said, when we'd driven a few hundred metres up the hill from the noodle shop. The building looked like a weatherboard version of the sheds used on construction sites. 'It used to be a piggery, but the Department of Livestock gave up on pigs.'

'Come on, Dominique.' Anna jumped out of the car. 'No time to waste. I have to show you and Phuentso what's left to do on the database.'

'Can you take care of yourself for a couple of hours?' Dominique asked me. 'Work finishes at four in the winter, so we won't be long.'

'Sure,' I said, disappointed. 'Where's the bathroom?'

'It'd be better to wait until we get home.' She lowered her voice. 'The toilets here aren't much better than on the trains in Romania.'

There, I hadn't been able to enter the cubicle without retching. 'I haven't been since I left the hotel at four this morning. Could I just go outside?'

'No. Be brave. Go out the door and left to the end.'

The toilet was a typical Asian squat model, which was usually quite hygienic if the men squatted even when they thought it wasn't absolutely necessary. From the stench and splatter marks, Dominique's colleagues clearly couldn't be bothered. I took a deep breath and rushed in. When my bladder was empty, I removed the small bucket from the larger one, scooped it full of water and tipped it over the toilet and surrounding area. I washed my hands from a tap directly over the bucket with a bar of soap I found on the floor.

Dominique gave me a questioning glance when I returned.

'It wasn't as bad as I was expecting from your description.'

She leaned away from the computer where Anna was pointing at a database screen. 'They wash the tea cups in that same bucket. Don't accept any tea.'

I sat down at Dominique's desk which, like the others, was partitioned into her own space. Dominique, who'd donned a fleece at the restaurant, had put another layer on when she arrived at the office. I sat huddled in my coat, thinking ten degrees had never felt so cold.

'There's a heater under the desk.'

I looked down to see an old radiator with the elements exposed. 'You'll catch fire if you try to use this.'

Dominique winced and lifted up her *kira* to show me the burnt hem.

An old woman in red and yellow robes walked past our bedroom window in the morning light, spinning a prayer wheel in one hand. Selden's grandmother, I assumed. I carried the last of my clothes to the wardrobe and placed them on the shelf Dominique had left for me. When I turned back, the woman had put down the prayer wheel and was pressing her forehead against the glass, cupping her hands around her face to see better. I rushed to the window and threw the curtains across, startled by the lack of respect for privacy.

With no food in the fridge, I was to join Dominique for another noodle lunch, so I headed outside and was immediately set upon by the Tibetan Mastiff tied up at the edge of the parking space. In size and colour, he appeared to be a small, exuberant yak. All around us were bare apple trees. The house was set in the middle of a sunny orchard, with the owners living upstairs and the renovated ground floor being rented out to expats. Until Anna moved in a few years ago, our flat had been the barn traditional in Bhutanese houses.

Alone on the hillside across the valley sat a monastery built by our landlord's ancestors. I noticed marijuana lining our switchback driveway as I descended, but it didn't seem to have ever been harvested. At the bottom, I turned away from town and walked along the road. Stray dogs barked as they moved to avoid me, then banded together to escort me beyond their territory. A man in an officer's uniform nodded at me as I passed an Indian army base. In fifteen minutes, I was at the restaurant.

'So, what do you think of Bhutan?' asked Phuentso, as I tucked into my bowl of noodles with egg.

'Beautiful country. Terrifying roads.' His expectant smile urged me to say more, but I was yet to experience much of the country and I didn't know these people well enough to ask if it was normal for old ladies to look into the bedroom windows of newly-weds. 'You studied in Australia, didn't you? What did you think of my country?'

He grinned. 'Beautiful country. Terrifying oceans.' He'd obviously picked up our humour.

'What were you studying?'

'Dairy technology. Making yoghurt, ice cream, that sort of thing.'

'Are you going to make those here?'

'Not as long as the current management's in place. They just want me to keep the computers working.'

'That's a waste. Can't you pull some strings? Dominique said you're related to the royal family.' I hoped I wasn't insulting him or his colleagues and his laugh put me at ease.

'Not that closely. I've got to put in the years like everyone else. In Bhutan, rights are all based on seniority.'

That sounded Japanese, or generally Asian, and it wasn't my place to question it, especially when Phuentso himself barely showed frustration. I searched for a way to change the topic until I knew the cultural terrain better and my eye fell on a newspaper sitting on the table. It was covered in squiggles similar to Sanskrit. 'Is that Dzongkha? What does it say?'

Dominique started laughing and leant over to whisper, 'Not everyone speaks Dzongkha.'

'I do speak Dzongkha.' Phuentso gave Dominique a mock glare. 'I just don't remember how to read it, that's all.' He looked back at me to explain. 'I was never very good at it at school and then when I went to High School in India, I lost it completely. English is much easier. Anyway, ask Dr. Dorji. It's his paper.'

Dr Dorji's nature matched his physique – small and unimposing. 'It's yesterday's paper, and this article,' he said, pointing to the small section on the front page under my finger, 'is about a bus accident in India. The Bhutan Post bus went off the road and killed two passengers.'

'If you think Bhutanese roads are bad,' said Anna, 'you should try driving in India. No one slows down for anything. The Bhutan Post bus is meant to be the safest way to travel to Kolkata, but this crash has scared everyone.'

Dominique whispered to me again. 'Anna's flying from Kolkata on Tuesday. She's meant to get there by a bus on that same line.'

'I don't drink beer.'

Dr. Wangdi's grin disappeared and I realised I'd offended one of Dominique's colleagues. Not a good way to start a Friday evening. He had a stocky build, rounded out further by a *gho*. He and the fifty other people gathered outside the pig sheds to bid Anna farewell all looked like they'd been out in the sun too long.

'Do you have something stronger?'

Grin restored, he put his arm around my shoulders and guided me round the unlit bonfire to the drinks table. 'Have you tried the local whisky?'

'Three brands of whisky?' I noted. 'Is this what Gross National Happiness means?'

That brought a laugh. 'No. To understand that, you need to try *ara*. It's the traditional alcohol in Bhutan.'

I took a whiff of the *ara*, my head jolting back as the fumes burnt through my sinuses, reaching for a direct attack on my brain. 'Let me start with the whisky.'

He poured me a shot of a brand I'd seen in the store yesterday and stood back to watch as I sipped it.

'It's delicious,' I said honestly. 'I'm no connoisseur, but this is better than anything I had even in Scotland. It's so smooth and warm.' I picked up the bottle to inspect the label.

FROM THE LAND OF THE GOLDEN DRAGON
SPECIAL
COURIER
WHISKY
BLENDED WITH VATTED MALT FROM SCOTLAND
42.8% V/V
Manufactured by:
GELEPHU DISTILLERY
(A unit of Army Welfare Project)

'It really is a Scottish malt,' I said. 'That explains the quality.'

'Yes, but it's distilled locally with fresh water from the Himalayas. That's the real quality.'

I read further. 'Army Welfare Project?'

Dr. Wangdi was enjoying my mirth. 'Is that strange?'

'Yes. First that a Buddhist country has an army. Second that the army has to raise its own welfare money. And mostly that a Buddhist army would use alcohol to do that.'

The smile stayed, but his eyes turned serious. 'What do you know of Buddhism?'

'Not much. I guess I see it as philosophy rather than religion with no gods to worship and being more inwardly focused on the role our own actions play in our lives. And that you respect all life to the point that you won't even kill mosquitoes.'

'You might find it's more complex than that.'

'I hope so. Anyway, I think that every country has the right to defend itself and if a side effect is that I get to drink whisky this good, I'm not complaining.'

Dr. Wangdi's eyes regained their humour and he looked about to respond, but some more people arrived. 'Excuse me. Some of my colleagues from the head office have arrived.'

I nodded and pulled my coat around me as he left. At five o'clock, the sun had already gone and my sheepskin-lined full-length Drizabone wasn't enough to keep me warm. How did Dr. Wangdi manage in a knee-length *gho*, even with thermal underwear? It must have had something to do with his stocky build.

I looked around for someone else to talk to, but as friendly as I knew everyone would be, my fear of meeting new people kept me near the drinks table. I'd watch for a while first.

'And this is Mr. Murray.' Dr. Wangdi brought the new arrivals across to serve them *ara*. 'He's here from Australia.'

'Will you be working at DoL?'

Dr. Wangdi translated for me. 'That's the Department of Livestock.'

'No,' I said. 'I'm a house husband.'

'*Doma?*' Dr. Norbu, Dominique's immediate boss and head of this pig shed, took out a packet containing betel nuts and leaves.

'Thanks.' I took one of the nut halves, white streaked with red, and held it in a leaf as he did.

'You smear the nut with this lime,' he told me, handing over a thimble full of white paste.

I copied his actions, scooping a bit up with the nut.

'Now put it all in the leaf and it's ready.' He popped it in his mouth to prove it.

I did the same. 'Do you chew it?' With the bundle in my cheek, it came out as a string of vowels.

'No, no,' he said urgently.

I considered the sensation, but the best analogy I could come up with was that it was like having a bunch of leaves in my mouth – leaves that slowly dissolved and trickled their juice down my throat. I didn't get the point.

'Come,' said Dr. Norbu. 'It's time.'

We joined the crowd gathered around the bonfire and watched Anna pull out her lighter and bend to the pile. Flames quickly licked up the chemically doused wood. A cheer went up to meet the 'whoomf' of the fire and talk immediately resumed, louder by at least the volume of the crackling.

Dominique appeared at my side. 'What are you drinking?'

'The best whisky I've ever had.' I offered it to her and watched her take a sip.

'You're right. It is good.' Dominique laughed as I staggered a step to put my arm around her shoulder, and she didn't seem to worry that the affection would offend her colleagues tonight. 'How much have you had?'

'I think it's only my second glass.'

She looked around. 'Have you met many people?'

'Quite a few. They all laugh when I tell them I'm your house husband. The joke gets funnier every time I say it.'

She frowned. 'Or with every sip of whisky.'

I took the point. 'What's up with this *doma*? My cheek's gone numb. Is that the idea?' I blanched as my probing tongue found a hole in the flesh that felt like it was about to meet open air. I quickly spat the *doma* out.

'What's wrong?' Dominique asked.

'The bloody *doma* thing just ate right through my cheek.'

She laughed. 'You're meant to chew it, you *stupidful*.'

'But Dr. Norbu told me not to.'

'I could barely understand you with that pile in your mouth. He probably thought you asked if you should swallow it.'

Dr. Norbu finished thanking Anna for her help over the last four years and gestured a request to expand the circle. 'Let's start with a dance everyone knows.'

The Bhutanese all faced the left and took a step as he started to sing, quickly adding their voices to his. I followed their feet, watching as they took three steps to the left, then turned back to the right for three steps then turned on the spot. Beside me, Dr. Wangdi noticed me trying to copy him.

'Don't look at me. I don't know the moves properly, either. Watch that woman over there. She's good.'

On the other side of the circle, Dominique was a step behind everyone else. This was her first time doing the traditional dances too. I found the woman my neighbour had indicated and watched her graceful moves, hands flowing from hip to shoulder height. There were none of the delicate finger motions of traditional Indian dances, but her hand positions hinted at what might be possible by a trained professional or by future generations building on current dances.

Just as I felt I was getting the hang of it, the dance ended and someone else began a new song with different steps. It took a couple of beats for everyone to catch up, but soon we were stepping in and out with similar arm movements.

The next dance had a salsa-like kick and the one following it involved clapping hands with others as in a children's game. With each dance, people became more involved and I was easily caught up in the joy of shared motion and the laughter at my own mistakes.

I tried to copy the expert, but lost track of my feet, tripping over Dr. Wangdi.

'See. It's harder than it looks.'

'How do you remember them all?'

'I've danced these at every party since I was a child, but it doesn't take long to get the basics. You'll have to lead one next time.'

Grocery vendors perched amid their stock on knee-high concrete slabs that ran the length of the weekend market. Permanent tin roofs stood over each row of concrete, awnings strung between them, presumably to protect the produce rather than the customers walking along the narrow dirt aisles.

'These grapes look good,' Dominique said, stopping in front of one seller who sat cross-legged on her section of the slab, surrounded by fruit. 'How much?'

The woman pointed at some pineapples on a tarpaulin.

'No, the grapes.' Dominique pointed at the lush bunches. 'How much?'

Ten fingers.

Dominique's lips moved quickly, counting in Bhutanese. 'Two kilograms, please. *Nee.*'

The seller smiled and placed two weights on one metal plate and began piling grapes on another. When she had a sizeable stack, she picked up the centre of the scales and added small bunches until the balance tipped in favour of the grapes. These she dumped into a bag I held out.

Dominique handed over the money. '*Kadin che.*'

'*Kadin che*,' the woman thanked us back.

'What about tomatoes?' I asked Dominique.

'It's not the season.'

I picked one up. 'Are you sure? They look beautiful.'

'Which means they must be imported from India and full of chemicals.' She marched off down the aisle and I hurried to follow, worried I'd lose her amongst the bustling colour. Most of the shoppers were women, wearing reds, greens and golds, all negotiating emphatically.

Dominique stopped near the end of the aisle. 'She wants five for those cucumbers, but she might be ripping us off because she thinks we're tourists.'

My arms were starting to tire from carrying the selection of fruit and vegetables, each in multiples of kilograms. 'We'll pick up the true value in time. As it is, we've got more than a week's worth of food for about five dollars. Just pay the money.'

'Murray, we need to be careful with our money until we can transfer more from Europe. We have to buy the car on goodwill as it is. Every ngultrum matters.'

We entered the landlord's apartment through the front door. A door on the opposite side of the entrance led to our own apartment, but we'd bolted the door on our side for privacy.

'Come in. Come in.' Kinley, the landlady, was farmer's-wife stocky with bright, friendly eyes and a matching smile. Her teeth were stained red from chewing *doma*. 'Leave your shoes on. It's fine.'

We took our shoes off anyway. It was clear from the boots crowding the entrance that they didn't wear shoes inside themselves. She led us up wooden stairs with a simple, elegant banister to a dark hallway stretching in both directions, then to a room at one end where her husband Kinga waited with another guest.

Kinga reached no higher than my shoulder, but there was a calm confidence in his stance that told of the strength of his character. I was immediately humbled. His smile as he shook my hand was not as free as his wife's, as though he was reserving judgement, and his eyes sparkled with intelligence rather than friendliness, but there was genuine warmth in his voice. 'Welcome to our house. We're sorry to lose Anna after so long together, but now we have two more people to help keep the house warm. You've met Dr. Norbu, of course.' The guest was Dominique's boss who I'd met the night before. There was a red hue to his lumpy face that suggested the glass in his hand wasn't his first.

'Yes,' he giggled, his mood expressed in the bounce of shoulders and squinting eyes. 'We met last night at Anna's farewell.'

'Did you know that Dr. Norbu studied in France?'

That hadn't come up in our *doma* conversation the previous night. 'No, I didn't. Your French must be much better than mine, then.'

He shook his head in an attempt at humility that was belied by his grin and bouncing shoulders.

'Please,' Kinga said, having greeted Dominique and Anna, 'take a seat.' He pointed us to a set of bench sofas arranged around a coffee table. It was a style that Anna had mimicked in our living room, but these were covered in brightly coloured woollen spreads where ours were bare cushions. Like the rest of the house, the walls were wood-panelled to shoulder height, but here, the white above was capped with cornices as colourfully decorated as the benches. A few photos of family members hung around the room, but pride of place was given to a photo of the King, high on the back wall. A small sign stating 'If you love your job, you need never work a day in your life' rested in a corner and a bunch of flowers sat on a table near the door.

'Would you like to try some Bhutanese wine?' asked Kinga.

'*Ara?*' I didn't want to offend our host and I knew I'd have to try it some time. It was probably best when I was only a few steps from home. 'I'd love to try some.'

Dominique prodded me. 'It's rude to accept straight away. You're meant to say '*meshu meshu*' at least twice before you accept.'

'And if I refuse a third time?'

'You won't be offered again.'

Kinga poured me half a tumbler and I sipped carefully. It tasted like Japanese *sake*, which I used to love until one evening I finished a whole bottle and spent the night throwing up. It seemed my body hadn't forgotten and I knew it was going to be difficult to get through the glass. I let the fumes make me cough so I'd have an excuse if I couldn't manage it. 'It's stro... ong, but good.'

'Dominique tells me that you work in Information Technology.'

'Yes, but more on the service management side. I'm not sure I'll be much help in Bhutan.'

'Oh, I'm sure you'll find a way to help in no time. I'm convinced that IT is the future of our country. We need to follow the example of India in that at least.'

'But you need to be able to feed yourselves first,' Dominique jumped in. She'd been doing her homework and knew that the balance of trade in agriculture was heavily in India's favour. 'You don't want to be relying on India forever.'

Intelligent eyes locked onto Dominique's. 'Do you think that's possible?' His tone expressed scepticism without being condescending. 'Much of Bhutan is too high or too steep for agriculture. How can we grow enough to feed one million people?'

'You might not be able to provide one hundred percent of the food you eat, but it should be possible to grow most of it, maybe three quarters.'

The conversation went on with Dominique sharing her belief that agricultural dependence led to economic blackmail and Kinga stating that self-sustenance was impossible, so why even bother trying. He believed it was better for Bhutan to develop its own economic power so they could buy whatever they needed. I found the reasoning of both sides to be strong and was unable to add much to the discussion. Surprisingly, neither did Dr. Norbu, though I was unsure whether that was out of respect to Kinga or lack of an opinion.

Anna also seemed to be sitting the discussion out. 'Where's Kinley?' I asked her. The hostess hadn't been in the room since we arrived.

'In Bhutan, the family don't eat with guests. Only the husband does.'

'Why's that?'

'I don't know the history, but it's the traditional division of roles. Cooking is the woman's job and entertaining is the man's.'

'So it's a patriarchal society, then. I guess that's to be expected.'

'No. Actually, most of the land is owned by women and is passed down to the eldest daughter.'

I mulled on that for a while, but couldn't make sense of it. Obviously there was a different definition of gender equality here to the one I was used to.

Finally, just as my stomach was beginning to rumble embarrassingly, Kinley appeared, moved the flowers off the table and began to cover it with pots. Neither Dr. Norbu nor the girls offered to help, so I remained in place.

'Please.' Kinga waved us up to the table.

Kinley stood by the table, explaining each dish as though serving a buffet in a restaurant. 'Two types of rice – the red rice is a speciality of Bhutan. So is *ema datshi*. Don't worry. I haven't used too many chillies.'

The news disappointed me. I loved chillies and wanted to test my palate against the masters.

'This one's called *phapsha pa* and this is beef. And the egg,' she said, pointing at the final dish, 'has *datshi* in it.'

Datshi meant cheese, which I wasn't fond of, so I went easy on the egg, but helped myself to plenty of the *ema datshi*. It seemed more like soup and the mass of chillies was sure to drown the cheese flavour. Everyone watched as I picked up the spoon and scooped a single chilli, tempered with a generous dose of rice.

'What do you think?' Kinga's curiosity seemed torn between hope that his guest didn't burn up and hope that the foreigner recognised the superiority of the Bhutanese in the chilli arena.

'It's great. I love—' To my humiliation, the last word was drowned in a hiccough.

'Now I don't feel so bad,' Dominique said, cutting her chillies with the spoon. 'The first time I had *ema*, I thought they were beans. I mean, who'd eat whole chillies like this? So I took a big spoonful.' She almost choked on her laughter at the memory. 'I didn't know what to do once I realised. I just had to chew it up and my face was all red.'

'Ah, we Bhutanese love chillies,' said Kinga. 'When I went to France, I really missed *ema datshi*. You just can't find chillies in France.'

He looked down to scoop up a decent amount of chillies to demonstrate and while his attention was on his food, Dominique dropped a piece of pork onto my plate. I glared at her and went to give it back, but Kinga was looking at us again. The '*pa*' in the dish called *phapsha pa*, I realised, must mean 'fat'. It was all pork, but only a scrap of each piece was meat. These pigs must have been force-fed to have so much fat.

'They feed them marijuana.'

I stifled a laugh as I realised that Anna was serious.

'It's true. They don't use it as a drug here. Most people wouldn't even know that's how we use it in other countries, but it grows everywhere, so they feed it to the pigs. It makes them hungry and lazy, perfect for producing lots of fat.'

'And Bhutanese people like that?'

Kinga didn't have any on his plate, but Dr. Norbu's shoulders bounced up and down as he spooned lumps of fat into his mouth.

'I'm a vegetarian,' Kinga told me, which struck me as appropriate for a Buddhist. 'You don't have to eat it. We know that *chilips* don't like much fat in their food.'

I took a small bite anyway, just on the off chance that it was different to pork fat in Australia. It wasn't and I had to work hard to keep the disgust from my expression. The beef was better, though unique in all my experiences. Even cooked, it was like jerky. Dominique, who normally loved meat, slipped a piece onto my plate again. I wasn't sure why. It took some chewing, but it had a good meaty flavour and not a scrap of fat in sight. And red rice complemented every dish, with a texture exactly like brown rice, but an unusual nutty taste.

'Please,' said Kinga, before I was even halfway through. 'Have some more.'

'I will, I will. It's delicious.' And so I did, taking a full second helping while everyone else placed a small picking on their plates. Again, before I was halfway through, Kinga urged me on to have thirds and Kinley stood in the doorway echoing him.

'Please have more. There's so much food left.' When I finally finished the second plate, I felt as if I was letting them down, but there wasn't any room for a single grain of rice more. It would be a relief to relax back into the sofa, but these benches had no backs.

'Well, you must be tired,' said Kinga. 'Thanks for coming.'

I looked at Dominique, lost. We'd only just finished eating, but she, Anna and Dr. Norbu were all rising with our host. I jumped to my feet and followed them all to the door. Kinga walked us downstairs where we picked up our shoes, stepped into the cold and headed round to our front door.

'What just happened?' I asked Dominique when we'd closed the door behind us. Anna was already packing in her room.

Dominique went to the kitchen to boil water for tea and a bed warmer as she answered. 'That's the Bhutanese way, it seems. Talk and talk and talk, then eat and leave. It's all a bit abrupt, but you'll get used to it. What did you think of the beef?'

'I thought it was fine. Why didn't you eat yours? Is there something wrong with it?'

'Oh, nothing probably.'

'Probably?'

'It's just that I don't really know where the meat comes from. They're Buddhist, so they don't want to kill the cows. That means that they probably died and I don't know if it was from old age or disease.'

The taxi I'd just flagged down pulled up in front of me. A middle-aged man in the passenger seat was chatting to the driver. I slid the back door open and ducked inside. A teenage girl wordlessly offered me some of her potato chips once I'd settled. Remembering my manners, I refused twice before accepting a small amount.

'*Kadin che.* Is it school holidays today?'

'No. I'm going to college now.'

'Are you eighteen already?'

'No. I didn't get the marks to continue to year eleven, so I'm studying finance instead.'

'Where do you do that?'

'At the Institute of Technology. They teach computer courses and how to use finance applications.'

The van began to shake, struggling up a hill. I looked to the front and noticed it was in third gear and the driver made no motion to drop it back down. My confidence in his ability shaken, I suddenly remembered the sheer drop just feet away. I forced my attention back to the conversation.

'What will you do when you finish?'

'I'll have to look for a job in a private company. The government employs most school leavers, but it's tough if you don't finish school. There aren't many jobs.'

The taxi slowed down outside the Bhutanese army barracks.

An army captain opened the door and sat down beside me. The girl leaned across to offer him some chips.

'Your English is very good,' I said to the girl. 'How come so many Bhutanese speak English?'

'All our school is in English because most of the teachers come from India.'

Having walked around town all day, I was enjoying some quiet time with new friends sitting on the grass of the swimming pool complex, playing idly with the stalks. All three men looked like Hollywood jocks, with tracksuits covering their muscly builds, but they all had open, friendly faces.

'Why don't you come along too?' asked Dema Wangchuk, the *taikwondo* instructor I'd just tracked down.

I plucked a blade of grass and began dissecting it. 'I've never done *taikwondo* and I'd love to learn, but Dominique won't let me join.'

'Why not? You said you'd done other martial arts, so I'm sure you'd learn quickly.'

'That's the problem. Dominique's worried that I'll catch her up and might even be better than her.'

The most heavily built of the three jumped in. 'You let a woman push you around?'

I laughed at his teasing tone. 'In this I do. She's entitled to her own activity. I'll find something else. I'm more interested in learning traditional archery anyway, since that's the national sport.'

'That's great. I haven't done archery in years.' Dema looked at the other two. 'Have you?'

They shook their heads.

'We could go shopping for the bows together and set up a target behind the gym. Then you wouldn't have to play in the public ranges. It's too dangerous for beginners. You might hit someone.'

'That'd be great. I'd love to do that, but give me some time to settle in.'

'You should come to the gym, too,' said the solid one. 'It's not much, but my friends and I meet up every afternoon to do body building. I could show you how to put on more muscle.'

'I'm not really into gyms. I'd rather do aerobic exercise.' I turned to the last of the three. 'What do you do?'

'I'm the assistant coach for the national basketball team.'

'I love basketball,' I said. 'Do you have any social competitions?'

'Sure. I'm just putting a team together now for one that's starting up soon. We'd love to have someone your height on the team.'

'Great. Count me in.'

'We start training next Wednesday. Come along at six p.m.'

'Will do. Dema, when do you want to see Dominique?'

'Bring her at the same time and I'll see what she knows.'

He neglected to mention that if he accepted her, Dominique would be training with the national team.

Dominique and I were in the middle of solving the problems of the world over dinner that evening when the power failed. Anna had already caught her bus, so we sat alone in the dark, scooping empty forks into our mouths and listening to rats war in the ceiling. We both jumped when the phone rang.

'Hello,' I said once I'd stumbled my way to pick it up.

I didn't understand a word of the Dzongkha that was fired down the line in a male voice, and I said so in English.

'You're a foreigner?'

'Yes.'

'Oh. How long have you been here?'

'Just a few days.'

'Welcome to Bhutan. What do you think of our country?'

I had no idea who was on the other end. 'It's beautiful and the people are very friendly.'

'Ah yes. It's true.'

Had I finally got the right answer or was this some telemarketer who'd do anything for a sale?

'Where are you from?'

'Australia.'

'I've heard it's a lovely place. What's your name?'

By now I was suspecting that it might even be a thief casing the joint. 'Who are you?'

'My name? You want to know my name?'

'Um... yes.' Though I wasn't sure it would help.

'I'm Dorji Wangchuk from Phuentsholing.'

I'd seen the town name on a sign near our house along with the number 247, which I assumed was the distance in kilometres. He gave me his phone number.

'If you have any trouble while you're in Bhutan or need something, just give me a call.'

'Who was that?' Dominique asked when I sat back down.

'Wrong number. But he offered his help if we need it. The people here are so friendly and helpful. It's an amazing country. I haven't seen any beggars. Everyone seems to be taken care of. They might have terrible roads and problems with water and electricity, but in every way that counts, Bhutan is the most civilised country I've ever been to.'

The warmth of the bar spilled out through the windows onto the freezing street. Dominique pushed open the door and we joined the thrum of expats and like-minded Bhutanese laughing and reviewing the week's frustrations. A couple of locals were smoking just inside the door.

'Probably friends of the owner,' said Dominique. 'Oh, look. Chris is here.' She introduced us, then ran off to get drinks.

Chris was a tall, neat Australian man my own age who was working at the government's Department of Information Technology. 'Dominique told me that you work in IT. Have you thought about helping out while you're here?'

'I'd love to, but I don't know that my expertise would be useful to anyone. I've been most involved with video-conferencing.'

His eyes widened. 'Really? We're doing a project now that will use that. We'd love to have you on board.'

'What are you doing exactly?'

'It's a showcase for the National Assembly to show them how IT can benefit the people and video-conferencing is the most impressive technology we could think of to wow them with, but none of us have ever used it before. There's a meeting on Wednesday. Would you be able to come along?'

'Sure. Will I need to wear a *gho*?'

'No. I normally just wear a suit.'

'I've only got jeans.'

'Then you will need a *gho* and because it's a building with a flag, you'll need to dress up with the *kabne* too.'

'What's a *kabne*?'

'It's a formal decoration for men, but it's hard to describe. Ask them to show you when you're buying your *gho*.'

The lady behind the counter ran her hand carelessly down piles of *ghos*. 'Sorry.'

'Can I get one in my size anywhere?'

Even her sneer lacked interest. 'Shop thirty two.'

'What country was *that* shop in?' asked Dominique as we began the search for number 32. When we found it, tucked between 27 and 18, it had all the selection and warmth that the other store was missing. Around the perimeter of the shop, *ghos* and *kiras* stacked shelves so densely that they spilt onto the floor and counter. The counter itself, running across the back and down both sides of the store, was almost submerged beneath *ghos* of maroon, navy and grey with gold embroidery, and *kiras* in myriad colours. The centre of the shop was filled with material ready for custom tailoring. We squeezed past other customers to reach a young man, who was restacking *ghos*.

'Yes, sir, of course we have something for you. Here, these are all extra large. Do you like any of them, sir?'

He made the usual noises of appreciation over our choices, then suggested that the check pattern of red, maroon and black, highlighted in yellow was a good choice. 'Sir, this one will make you look Bhutanese.'

That settled it for me. 'Can I try it on?'

I put up with being called 'sir' for half an hour as the assistant put the robe on me and pulled and tucked the material to make sure it was right. All business in the shop stopped as other buyers watched the show. I stared back. Men appeared relaxed and dignified, women as elegant and graceful as catwalk models.

I asked the shopkeeper to teach me how to put the *gho* on myself and he rushed off to get a *tego*, a buttonless cotton garment with the same name as the women's outer blouse. Men wore a shorter, white version against their skin. While the women closed theirs with a brooch, one of the men watching pointed out that he paperclipped his to the *gho* to hold it in place. Unfolded, the sleeves of both *tego* and *gho* fell past my fingertips, but they folded back to form a cuff a hand-span wide. The *gho* was made in three equal parts so that the front flaps folded across each other to join the far seam and that was how I started. Holding the seams in place, the thing was so wide that my arms were stretched out at forty-five degrees and the hem was dragging on the floor.

'Dumbledore,' Dominique called from the audience and I could imagine that was just how I looked.

Still gripping the seams, I had to lift everything up so that the hem was at knee-height, exposing my jeans beneath.

'The Code of Conduct says that you should have the hem above your knees,' the shopkeeper told me.

'But it looks better below the knees, don't you think?' One man spoke for the men in the crowd, who all had their hems covering their knees.

'Only the king is allowed to have it lower,' said my dresser. I realised he was probably pushing the point because even the largest *gho* they had was a little short for me. Once the robe was pulled up and wrapped around the back so the spare material was pleated behind me, he wrapped a multicoloured thread belt, called a *kera*, around so tightly that even shallow breaths were painful. I couldn't see how the pleats and belt could be set with anything less than four hands, but they assured me I would get used to it. The excess material hung over the belt forming what the shopkeeper called 'the world's largest pocket'.

The onlookers clapped and spoke in unison. 'You look very smart.'

The *gho*, *tego* and *kera* came to just over one thousand ngultrum, less than the price of a t-shirt at home. Then I bought knee-length socks which were pulled up to meet the hem of the *gho*.

I had to get the formal *kabne* from a tourist shop, possibly because I needed a longer one than most people to cope with my height. It was a strip of off-white cloth about three metres by eighty centimetres and looked to be made of hemp. The saleslady couldn't show me how to wear it.

'I'm sorry sir. You'll have to ask a man to show you.'

I stood at the base of the cliff, belaying Dominique.

Robin, a Southern Bhutanese and head of the rock climbing club, was shouting her up the rockface, his style a mixture of encouragement and abuse – part concerned parent, part drill sergeant. He turned to me. 'She's not bad.' The double entendre was typical of Robin's cheeky sense of humour.

'Hey, get your eyes off my wife. Anyway, I thought you were married yourself.'

'I'm MBA.'

'What's that?'

'Married But Available. No one in Bhutan is really married.'

'What do you mean?'

'Only the really rich people bother signing contracts and making lifelong commitments. The rest of us just agree to be together.'

I could feel Dominique's tension in the stillness of the rope. She would also be wondering why we'd had to get married. I was fully committed to our relationship, but it would have made things a lot easier if we could have taken it at our own pace. Dominique still hadn't even found the courage to tell her friends we'd done it.

'How does that work? You just move in together?'

'If the man is still there in the morning, everyone considers them married.'

'Still there? You mean if a couple falls asleep after sex, they're married?'

'Not quite. Haven't you heard of night hunting?'

'The living legend,' said Nado. He was another climber, married to a French teacher who decided to stay, though I was no longer sure what their marriage entailed.

Robin saw my blank stare and explained. 'We don't have the sexual hangups that *chilips* have. If a boy likes a girl, he climbs in her window and spends the night with her, often in the same room as the family. That's called night hunting. If he's still there in the morning, they're married.'

'What happens if she gets pregnant and the boy leaves?'

'The family helps raise the baby. So will the next man, if he decides to stay.'

Nado was delighted by my shock. 'Don't ever leave Dominique alone at night.'

I rose to give Dominique a hug as she came through the door, but she brushed past me.

'I'm not in the mood. I've been hearing about Anna all day.' Her voice rose to a whine as she stamped down the hall. 'Anna could speak Nepali and Dzongkha. Anna would have lent me money. Anna made good Bhutanese food. Anna, Anna, Anna.'

I watched her take off her *tego* and unwind the *kera*. She exhaled, that one sigh seeming to carry the whole day's woes.

'They say it's the best part of the day – taking off this belt.'

'You know your colleagues aren't being fair, Dominique, so don't listen to them. We've only been here a couple of weeks. How can they compare you to Anna who'd been here for four years and was in Nepal before that?'

'It doesn't matter how. They do. And Dr. Norbu always tells me how good a worker she was and how he wishes she was still here. Well, so do I. We should never have come.'

On Monday morning, only two weeks after I arrived, I gave in to Dominique's demands that I get a local driving licence. I told myself it wouldn't be so scary if I was at the wheel, but I wasn't sure I believed it. To get to town, I decided to try walking the new highway that they were constructing on the valley floor. Along the way, I passed men and women – often with children on their backs – carrying bags of cement, breaking rocks with sledgehammers and shifting piles of dirt. They looked up and smiled amongst themselves as I passed and I assumed it was in appreciation of my new *gho*. I'd spent an hour putting it on myself that morning. I'd tried sitting down. I'd tried holding everything in place against a wall. In the end, just as frustration was about to get the better of me, I'd tried clothes pegs. I was happy with the result and enjoyed the recognition of my effort. For an hour, I returned smiles and tried to give them encouragement for their hard work, but by the end, I started to wonder whether they might actually be laughing at me.

The Road Safety & Transport Authority was on our side of the river, just before town. A crowd stood before the counter and I patiently waited my turn, but a young man saw me and beckoned me into the office interior. Half the crowd outside followed me in, all pushing their own papers forth.

'We don't get so many *chilips* in here,' he said. 'What do you need?'

I explained my purpose and he handed me the necessary papers, indicating that I should fill them out leaning over his desk. Somehow, he managed to ignore the press of people behind me.

'You need to fill in your blood type.'

'I don't know what it is.'

He looked at me with incredulity and I remembered that in Asia, not knowing your blood type is like not knowing your star sign. I could have made it up, but I wasn't even sure what the options were. Besides, it could make a small disaster worse at some point in the future, so I held out.

'Well, you'll have to get it checked at the hospital. I can't give you a licence until we know your blood type.'

He explained the way to the hospital and I climbed up the hill on the other side of Thimphu. The road took me past a *chorten* over ten metres high. The Buddhist monument, a white sculpted mud pillar, was being circled by pilgrims trying to improve their *karma*. The ten-metre square base supported a bulb that tapered to a shaped spire. Each of the people I passed laughed and smiled at me and I took it more personally each time. I looked down at my *gho*, but I couldn't see anything wrong. It wasn't like

I'd come out without my underwear. In fact, I had my jeans on against the cold. What were they laughing at?

Finally I reached a three-storey building surrounded by construction. A large sign labelled it the 'Jigme Dorji Wangchuk National Referral Hospital.' Inside, another sign requested that visitors not spit, but familiar red splotches abounded on the floor. The crowd in front of the reception desk was playing the 'longest arm, first served' queuing game, young men showing no regard for the hunched old ladies in front of them. My arms were probably longer than everyone else's but I had no idea where they got the forms they were proffering. Still, when in Thimphu... I joined the press and was soon near the front. The nurse behind the counter blinked when she saw me and served me before the waiting masses.

'Name, age and nationality?'

'Murray Gunn.' I watched her write it in Dzongkha. 'Thirty three. Australian.'

'Address?'

'Um. Near the Indian army camps about eight kilometres from here towards Paro.'

'Thimphu,' she said, accepting the name of the capital as my official address. 'Take this form and start with an eye and ear test. Go up the stairs to room five.'

I spent two hours getting various tests done before being directed to the blood test counter, then waiting in front of a doctor's room for a signature. There, I practised the Bhutanese style of queuing and got a nurse's attention.

'There aren't enough doctors on duty today.' She threw my form back at me. 'Go up to the top floor and see the director.'

The director's secretary seemed a bit more organised and numbered everyone's forms. When it was nearly my turn, I was waved into the reception area and sat down.

One of the other patients grabbed my form. 'What are you here for?'

I took hold of the paper and pulled gently until he let go. 'I just need this form signed.'

'Well, don't wait out here. Just go in.'

I didn't like getting special treatment because I was a foreigner, but someone else pushed past the crowd and through the door, so I followed them. There was another crowd inside. The director sat behind a large wooden desk, facing a middle-aged man in a shabby *gho* standing on the opposite side. Both men looked up at my entrance, but continued their conversation. The director spoke only in English, despite the fact that the patient always replied in Dzongkha.

'I'm sorry, but we can't refer you to India until we can prove it is testicular cancer.'

'I understand your situation, but I can't do anything more now. You'll just have to wait until the testicle scans come back.'

The director managed to insert the word 'testicle' into almost every sentence and I began to wonder if he was deliberately speaking English to make the patient uncomfortable so he'd leave quickly. The tactic didn't work as well as he might have hoped and it was five minutes before the farmer trod wearily past me. The director waved me over and asked for my form.

'You haven't filled in this part. What's your distinguishing feature?'

'I'm not sure what you're after.'

'A mark. A mole. Something that's unique to you. Something the police can use to identify you.'

His casualness was haunting, giving me the impression that they expected road accidents here. And I wasn't going to tell him where my mole was. Not in front of this room full of people. But I had a marriage to maintain. 'Blue eyes?'

He didn't even smirk. 'What's that above your lip? Is that a mole?'

I ran my fingers over my lip and found a bump. It was a pimple, but I agreed that it probably was a mole and I was released.

The Road Safety & Transport Authority had closed for lunch by the time I got back, so I pulled out the *Lonely Planet* to find somewhere to eat. I chose a café overlooking a roundabout where a policeman directed traffic, cars carefully negotiating the pack of stray dogs lying in the middle of the intersection. The café was a pen for tourists herded by their guides, which wasn't how I liked to travel so I left as soon as I'd finished eating.

When the RSTA reopened, the young man looked at my form and laughed.

'You only needed to find out your blood type. This form is for people going for a *new* licence. Anyway, I can't take your application until you've paid the fees and the cashier is only open in the mornings.'

I'd also come prepared to get our visas made official. The Ministry of Foreign Affairs looked almost as much like a castle as the *dzong* across the river. It was a long walk from town, but they quickly sorted out our visas. Unfortunately, they told me I also needed to get a non-citizen resident permit, but couldn't tell me what documentation I would need for that.

I headed back into town to the government offices. Each was a single-storeyed whitewashed mud house. Inside the Department of Immigration, I explained my need and the girl at the counter beckoned me to follow her. She took me out to the back offices where she relieved her colleague, smoothly taking over the game of solitaire he was playing.

The colleague gave me a form and listed the other three documents I'd need to gather in my quest. As he talked, his eyes slipped back to the game. I left him to wrest control of the computer back from the woman and made my weary way home.

This time I found the stand for taxis that went along our road and asked for someone to take me to the Indian army barracks. One of the drivers grinned hungrily and directed me to his van. He opened the door for me before getting into the driver's seat.

'Wait. Aren't you going to take other people?'

'Oh.' His grin vanished. ' Don't you want reserved?'

'No. I want to share a taxi like everyone else.'

He pointed me to another microbus with a couple of people already on the back seat. I sat in the front, Australian style, and waited a few minutes for the fourth person.

I found that chatting to the driver helped distract me from the sheer cliffs beside the road. He told me that I should ask for Babesa, which was the end of the line for certain taxis on our route. If I asked for a specific village, then they'd want to give me a whole taxi to myself and charge for four seats.

Dominique was home when I arrived.

'You're wearing your *gho*.'

I grinned in reply, just holding back a proud 'and I put it on by myself.'

Then she burst out laughing. 'And you're wearing jeans. You can't wear jeans with a *gho*.'

So that's what everyone had been laughing at. 'But the *Lonely Planet* says you can.'

'Sure. If you're a farmer. And look at that hem line. You can't have the inside hanging down further than the outside. It looks terrible. Don't you know it's the first thing anyone will look at? The whole town must have been laughing at you.'

Dominique sat opposite me at the table in our study. She'd been working on her database all evening, her muttering darker by the hour.

'Murray, does this make sense to you?'

'What's up?'

'Dr. Norbu hasn't even seen it, but he keeps telling me that the database is ready to use and to just create the training, but I don't get it. Look, each of these rows is a cow and all its information, but how will the program know which cow was the mother?'

I walked around the table and looked over her shoulder.

'Is that the whole thing? That's not a database. It's a table. What if the cow has more than three calves? Who put this together?'

'Anna had an Indian programmer do it. She used her own money. *Putain!* Can it be fixed?'

'I don't think it can be without starting again. I might be able to do it for you, but I'd want to use open source web technologies.'

'No. It needs to be done so that someone can change it after I leave. I'll talk to Dr. Norbu about getting some proper IT support. Then, hopefully, I can get on with doing something useful.' She let out a long breath, then looked up at me. 'Let's get dinner. What do you feel like?'

'Chilli con carne.'

'As if. Rice and veggies again?'

When Wednesday arrived, I was dreading the *gho*. Dominique refused to help me, saying that I needed to learn to do it myself just as she'd had to learn to put the *kira* on by herself. I had to admit that the *kira*, with its concertina folds, looked more complex than the *gho*, but the advantage was that most of the complexity was in front and I'd seen Dominique use her teeth to good effect. Most of the difficult adjustments for the *gho* occurred behind the back where I couldn't see, had less dexterity and no biting appendages. Again, I tried using the wall, sitting down, using pegs and paper clips, but that seam always hung down the front. After an hour I gave in and pulled the material up from the inside. It bundled uncomfortably between my knees, but it looked passable in the mirror. I added paper and pen to the pocket, along with the three-metre *kabne*, which gave me a Bhutanese stockiness.

My reflection in the mirror made me laugh. Above the bulk of the *gho*, my head looked like a point. With my arms folded, the sleeves flared out, then cut back to meet the bulk above the belt. That flared out and cut back again to the skirt, which flared out yet again. All this over skinny legs reaching down to heavy walking boots. It was the shape of a Christmas tree in a bucket.

I took a taxi to the RSTA to sort out my licence, then walked the length of town to the DIT offices. People stared but no one laughed and I began to relax until a man stopped in front of me and held his hand up to bar my way. A face showing signs of age poked out of a *gho* faded and rough with many washes. He walked with a staff, but he stood tall. The hand turned, his thumb rubbing across his fingers in the international sign for money. Disgusted, I stepped around him and went on my way.

Three young men stood chatting on the terrace in front of the flagged building.

'You look very smart.' The rehearsed manner of all three speaking the same words made them feel false.

I checked that I was in the right place before asking for help with my *kabne*. Yeshey, a man of about thirty years old, wearing a solid grey *gho* with the *kabne* looped around his shoulders, agreed to show me and the others jumped to help. One end folded into the other at the left shoulder, leaving the middle draped around the right hip just so and a tail falling down my back. The effect was something like a full-body lanyard.

More people arrived from various ministries, all telling me I looked smart, but the cloth of the *gho* rubbing between my knees made me feel a fraud. Eventually, the terrace became too crowded and we moved inside to our seats. The DIT director sat alone at the head table and called the meeting to order. I looked around the room, but realised that I was the only one not paying complete attention to the director and quickly looked back. A string of ums and ahs provided a beat to break up his stilted speech.

'I would like to take this chance to cordially welcome you all to the Department of Information Technology on this day. We are most fortunate to have representatives from the departments of agriculture, education and health attending today's meeting, as well as an Australian who's joining us in an independent capacity. Please extend your warm courtesy to him as he brings to the table a wealth of experience in video-conferencing.'

I felt myself flush as every eye in the room followed the direction of his gesture.

'This meeting has been called to formally kick off the showcasing project. All our distinguished guests would be aware that the esteemed National Assembly will be convening in Thimphu in June. It is our heartfelt desire to demonstrate to our exalted leaders the power of IT.

'You would all be aware that Bhutan only embraced the television and the internet in 1999. We remain behind the rest of the world but aim to catch up in haste. It is our express desire at this time to demonstrate video-conferencing to show how this technology can support the people of Bhutan in their daily lives. I would request that each of you consider ways we can demonstrate this.' He looked across at me. 'Does our esteemed colleague from Australia wish to say something?'

I realised I was fidgeting and felt like a six-year-old caught talking in class. No one else had spoken since the director opened the meeting. Should I say what was on my mind or try to shrug it off as the teacher's imagination?

'I'm sorry. It's just that I wonder whether video-conferencing is the right tool.'

Beside me, Chris spoke under his breath. 'He's a director. Call him *Dasho*.'

'*Dasho*, I know Bhutan's low population density and mountainous terrain make it difficult to create a high-speed network, but you just don't have the infrastructure to support video-conferencing.'

'*La*.' Chris added the honorific for me.

'Thank you for your considered words. Please allow me to inform you that it is not our intention to show what can be done now. Our purpose is to inspire our leaders to make best use of IT when creating their vision of the future Bhutan.'

I wasn't convinced. Video-conferencing took a lot of money and design to be useful. Jumping at a sexy technology seemed the classic case of choosing problems to fit the technology, rather than finding technologies to solve the biggest problems and I couldn't imagine the National Assembly would be impressed, but I realised that DIT was determined to do it so I might as well help them do it properly.

Not long after the group began to brainstorm ideas for how technology could be demonstrated, the director made his apologies. He announced Yeshey, the young man I met on arrival, as his replacement. Everyone remained silent as the director departed and Yeshey made his way to the head table.

'Mr. Chairman *la*.'

Yeshey acknowledged the speaker.

'Mr Chairman *la*, I propose that we break into groups to discuss the ideas for each of the chosen areas *la*.'

Yeshey agreed and presided over the choosing of groups. I wound up being a resource for every team. By the end of the session, the education group had decided to show how remote students could attend classes in the larger towns without leaving their villages; the health group had chosen to show how a doctor could diagnose a patient in a remote town; and the agriculture group planned to give farmers a view of road conditions so they could plan their trip to market.

Yeshey called the entire meeting back together, formally asking each group to present its plan and accepting a proposal that teams meet once a week to make their project happen. Once again, I made myself available to every group as they required.

As soon as Yeshey closed the meeting, the babble began again and he was at the centre of it.

'You should have worn your best *gho* today, Yeshey.'

'Aren't you the high and mighty?'

'Don't get ideas above your station.'

He took the teasing good-naturedly. 'This *is* my best *gho*.'

Dominique and I were going to the youth centre that evening and I was meant to meet her there, but I thought I was early enough to catch her on her way into town. I walked down to the bridge and watched a policeman watch traffic. He approached when he saw me, blue uniform snapping with starch as he walked, a lanyard tight around his left shoulder. He wore a white helmet labelled 'TRAFFIC.'

'Hello, sir. Are you lost?'

'No. I'm just waiting for my wife.'

'She's driving? Ah, you must be working in Bhutan.'

'My wife is.'

'What does she do?'

He was impressed when I explained. 'It's good that people like sir and his wife come to help our country. Education here is not as good as in your country and it's difficult for us. We have to walk a long way to school and we have to help our families. I wanted to go to university like sir, but I didn't get high enough marks to finish school.'

He was facing the traffic as he talked and I wondered what he was watching for.

'But you found a good job anyway. Do you like being a policeman?'

'I like it, but it's very hard. We have to stand up all day. Then after dinner, we go out again for night duty.'

Dominique and I had often been stopped when we came to town in the evening. The police had generally set up a checkpoint on the road to our home, checking licences. I asked him why?

'No one who drives in the evening has a licence.'

'No one?'

'Not many. They think it doesn't matter when there's not much traffic.'

'Do you only do traffic duty?'

'Yes. There are four sections of police, but we only do one.'

'What are the other sections?'

'Fire and rescue, *dzong* security and VIP security. The security sections both have rifles, but we're the only ones with helmets. Excuse me, sir.'

He raced across the road, leaving me to chuckle to myself over his pride in a hard hat. A car coming out of a side street halted when the blue uniform landed in its path. It was a new intersection. The signs had gone up on their poles last weekend, along with the arrows on the tarmac. After a few minutes of conversation through the window, the driver backed the car up the road and my new friend returned.

'Bhutanese people don't understand the road rules,' he said.

'But what did he do wrong? He was obeying all the signs.'

The policeman rolled his eyes. 'They don't apply until next Monday.'

Dominique was nervous when she headed off for her test with the *taikwondo* instructor. I bade her good luck, but privately wished that she'd find some confidence in herself. She had a blue belt and a passion for the sport, both of which would count for a lot. It didn't occur to me to be worried about myself.

Jamso introduced me to his friends as soon as I arrived at the gym. They were milling around practising shooting baskets. I changed quickly and joined them. My own shooting needed a lot of work, but it was the lack of oxygen that let me down. Jamso called us together and set us running up and down the court. By the time I returned to the starting point, I was winded. The next five laps of sidesteps and running backwards had my legs so full of liquid fire that I could barely stagger to where the others were gathered to wait for me. I was relieved to see that they were all puffing now too, but I was still the only one near collapse.

After setting the team to some fast-paced passing practice, Jamso bent down next to me to make sure I was okay. I managed to nod, then gasped out that I needed a few minutes. When I recovered, I joined the team for the last of the passing and had enough breath left to begin a practice game.

Jamso showed his skill, stealing the ball often and getting a basket every time he touched it. I spent most of my time spinning and falling, but managed to get a few baskets of my own. Increasingly, the figures around me blurred and my balance failed. I finally had to drag myself to the sideline and admit that two weeks wasn't enough time to acclimatise to the altitude when we were living in a town higher than any point in Australia.

My team let me go when Dominique appeared but made it clear they expected me to be fitter when I came back the following week. Dominique was also exhausted, but she hadn't been running for the last hour and still had enough breath to talk all the way home. She'd discovered that Dema was coaching the national team because she'd been surrounded by black belts, mostly in their teens and all very dedicated to *taikwondo*. They lived on site and trained up to six hours each day, but were happy for Dominique to join for a two-hour session twice each week.

When I swung my feet to the floor the next morning, pain jarred my left knee. I looked down at the swelling and realised that jeans wouldn't be an option for a few days.

On Friday night, I awoke to a scuffling sound. Knowing Dominique regularly made trips to the bathroom during the night, I snuggled back under the covers and drifted off to sleep again. I was just settling into nightmares of turning up to the office with no underwear under my *gho* when Dominique landed on me.

'Murray. Murray. ... *dans la chambre.*'

The pain of bones grinding in my knee made it difficult to follow her babble, but I understood that she'd heard the same sound and had gone to check what it was.

She switched to English. 'It's a rat. It's in our room.'

'Okay. Okay.' I got up and stumbled to the light switch, but by that time the rat was gone. It had probably scurried off in fright when Dominique jumped.

She was sitting in the middle of the bed, hugging the quilt around her. 'It was bad enough that they were in the roof, but I don't want them in our room.'

Having a pretty woman jump onto me in the middle of the night might have seemed like a great thing a month before, but my knee wouldn't stand for it now. The rats had to go.

'I saw some rat traps under the sink,' I said, climbing back into bed and wrestling the quilt from Dominique.

'Anna probably brought them over. I'll set them up tomorrow.'

I finally freed a corner of the cover and curled up under it. 'Are you sure that won't be disrespectful to the Bhutanese culture?'

'I'm not feeling very Buddhist tonight.'

Selden often returned to Thimphu for the weekend, so we invited her and her parents to dinner on Saturday evening. Kinga was very interested in my new project.

'I think IT is the way forward for Bhutan. It would be great if the National Assembly provided more money for technology. At the Chamber of Commerce, we're trying to set up some call centre companies like they have in India.'

'Is Bhutan ready for that?' I asked. 'The phone costs here are so high.'

'They won't come down unless we use them more. This would provide jobs, help build the economy, build infrastructure and reduce call costs all at the same time.'

Dominique sat on her hands and I knew that she was trying not to offend our guests by arguing again for the need to strengthen the agriculture sector rather than modernising so quickly.

I changed the subject. 'Kinga, a man stopped me in the street the other day and did this.' I copied the gesture of rubbing fingers with my thumb. 'What does that mean?'

'He was probably asking for money.'

'I thought begging was illegal in Bhutan. Was I wrong?'

Selden had been quiet for most of the evening, but she provided the answer. 'He was probably a monk. Some monks don't wear the red robes and it's not begging if you're a monk.'

She turned to Dominique while I tried to tackle her logic. 'By the way, have you heard from Anna?'

'Yes,' Dominique told them. 'She made it back to France. She'll be there for a couple of weeks before she starts her PhD.'

'She'll have a nice time in her parents' house,' said Kinga. 'It's such a beautiful place. I went to see them, you know, last time I was in France.'

'I miss her. She was like a part of the family.' It was clear that Kinley used to mother her. 'She used to come and have dinner with us all the time.'

I put my hand on Dominique's. This gathering wasn't going well for her. She'd see every topic as a comment on her worth, finding her lacking. I was searching for a way to change the subject when the rats began their nightly war.

Kinga looked horrified. 'Is it always like this?'

'All day and all night. Don't you hear it upstairs?'

'No, we don't. But if they eat too many holes in the walls, the house will fall down. You need a cat. Anna had a cat.'

Dominique and I talked over each other in our haste to crush this idea. We were both dog people. 'She also had some rat traps. We were thinking of putting them out. What do you think?'

'Oh, no. You can't. It will be bad for your *karma*.'

But not for the cat's, apparently. And while using rat traps to kill rats was bad for my *karma*, keeping a cat for the same purpose wasn't.

I saw Dominique stumble on her way to the door and jumped up to meet her. She stopped on the front steps, looking at the ground.

'Are you alright?'

When she looked up, her face was as white as a *geisha's*.

'I'm fine. I went to the hospital this afternoon to visit a colleague.'

I asked her to tell me about it and guided her inside. She sank down onto the cushioned bench and lay back.

'You know the girl I told you about, who's been off with stomach aches?'

I nodded, vaguely recalling Dominique's concern about a colleague who was away sick every second day.

'Well, her husband thought that the doctors were ignoring her because she was Southern Bhutanese. Today he started shouting at one of the doctors, demanding that they do some proper tests rather than just giving her digestion pills.' She closed her eyes and paled further. If she hadn't been lying down, I think my gutsy little wife would have fainted. 'They took an X-ray and found something stuck in one of her tubes. They operated immediately. It was a foetus. One of the doctors apparently said that if they hadn't operated, she might have died within a few hours.'

I remembered the queues I'd seen at the hospital and wasn't surprised by the doctor's efforts to minimise their work. Medical care was free even for foreigners, but at what cost?

'Is she going to be okay?'

'They say she'll be fine. She looked much better when we saw her.'

'Then what's affected you so badly?'

'You haven't seen the wards yet, have you? They're not like in hospitals in France, smelling of disinfectant. The rooms here are full of the stench of sick people and there isn't enough air. I fainted. My colleagues dragged me outside, I think. I might have walked myself – I don't know. But they had to pick me up off the floor. It was embarrassing.'

I patted her knee. What more could I do?

'They don't even feed the patients. Friends and family have to bring food for them. That's partly why we went – because her husband wouldn't leave her bedside to get food.'

'Speaking of food, you could probably do with some now to put colour back in your face.'

She groaned. 'I couldn't stomach rice and veggies right now.'

I answered a knock at the door to find Kinley holding a three-week-old kitten.

'I found you a cat.' She gave it a last pat and put it on the threshold, then pointed to a wide, low pot full of dirt she'd prepared. 'You'll need this. The cat will know what to do.'

'Dominique.' My voice faltered. 'Dominique!'

Kinley didn't wait for Dominique to arrive. 'Anna used to feed her cat tinned fish and rice.'

I closed the door behind her and turned to see Dominique looking at the cat with the horror I felt.

She looked up at me. 'We've got a cat,' we said in unison, then collapsed laughing, both in shock.

The cat began to explore its new home.

Dominique burst through the front door and charged down the hall to the bedroom. I put my book down, pushed Paprika off my lap, ignoring the cat's yowl, and rushed to her. She was quivering.

'What's wrong?'

Anger turned to sobs as she buried herself in my embrace. 'Dr. Wangdi...' She gasped a breath and used my shirt to wipe her tears, then had another go with no more success.

I held her tight and made calming noises until she could continue.

'We were starting to work well together. I was at his office to discuss progress on the database and he was really interested. I stayed late to explain some of the issues to him and he had great ideas. But then when I got up to go, he put his arm around me and kissed me.' She began sobbing again.

'It was vile. His teeth were all red and he stank of *doma*. Why does this always happen to me? In every country I work in?'

I wanted to rush down and confront him myself, but held back. Dominique would consider that further humiliation.

'Just because Anna went out with him, he thinks every French volunteer is his toy.'

'Anna went out with him? I thought he was married.'

'You know how it works. Married but available.'

I gave up trying to push Paprika off my keyboard and placed him on the ground where he sat wailing. My science fiction story was giving me trouble, but I was delighted to have the time to dedicate to it – or I would have been, if the cat didn't keep adding q's to my dialogue. The front door opened just as I was about to start typing again. It was too early for Dominique to come home and I hadn't seen her car arrive. I started getting up to see who it was, but stopped when Kinley's mother walked past the study, right into our hallway. I sat, stunned, as her footsteps continued on to the kitchen, then came back again. Seeing me gaping at her, she smiled, held up the plastic bags she'd fetched and stepped back outside, closing the door behind her.

I turned up at the Ministry of Education to join a showcase meeting, but found that their building had a flag out the front. That meant that I had to be wearing a *kabne* to enter and I'd forgotten to bring mine. I waited outside for ten minutes, hoping that someone would come past and carry a message to the team members for me, but no one did.

The situation was ironic. If I'd turned up in jeans, I wouldn't have been breaking the rules, but because I came in *gho*, I'd be considered under-dressed. If I went in, the Bhutanese might just say that I was an ignorant *chilip* and think nothing of it, but I didn't like breaking their customs. And there wasn't enough time to get home and back again before the meeting finished. In the end, I decided that respecting the culture was more important than keeping my appointment and headed off to DIT to see if I could help the team there.

When I arrived, Yeshey and his colleagues were heading for an early lunch and invited me to join them. The DIT canteen was a dingy couple of rooms below the meeting hall. Yeshey led me through to the kitchen and greeted a couple of chefs in white aprons. They didn't object when he started pulling lids off pots. '*Ema datshi, kewa datshi, dhal, phapsha pa*,' he recited as each dish appeared. 'Which one do you want?'

'Can't I have a try of all of them?'

'Sure.' Yeshey relayed my order to the kitchen staff and added his own.

We sat in the front room at a plastic outdoor setting. The paint on the cracked mud walls was faded. The lone decoration was a large photo of the king and a monk in a yellow sash.

'Is that the head lama?'

'That's Gendun Rinchen and, yes, he was the Je Kempo, but he passed away recently.'

Our food arrived and I realised that I'd broken protocol. Each dish came in its own small bowl and every person at our table had one curry and one *dhal* to go with their plate of rice. I had three curries ranged in front of me, as well as the *dhal* and rice. There was nothing for it but to try to eat them all, mostly chilli as they were.

'Dominique went to see a lama who died recently,' I told him. 'It was in a monastery near our place. She said that they'd put him in a meditation pose for everyone to view him.'

'I know the one you mean. He died in that pose. High lamas know when they're going to die and can meditate into the next life. The really good ones stay like that for days before their body decomposes enough that they fall down. Gendun Rinchen was very accomplished. He stayed sitting up for weeks and parts of his body were still warm days after he died. When his body still hadn't collapsed after a month – apparently he didn't even smell – they decided to put him in a *chorten* as a holy relic.'

'Where were you today?' I asked.

The French ambassador was in town and Dominique had been accompanying him all week.

'We went with all the other delegations and had an audience with the king.' Her voice rose an octave when she continued. 'He's even more handsome than the pictures.' A girlish sigh gave the claim more power. Had she ever spoken about me that way?

'Is he as wise as everyone says?'

'He seemed to be. All the ambassadors and their advisors asked interesting questions about the current five year plan and about Gross National Happiness and the king and his staff had very intelligent answers. It's easy to see why his people love him so much. It's almost like he runs the country by himself. It's unfair for one man to be so great.'

Great enough to keep four wives happy, I thought, while I had trouble with just one.

Dominique and I drove up to Dochu La, the first pass on the road to the east. It was shrouded in mist, as it had been every time Dominique had come this way with her colleagues. The road divided around a small hill in the middle of the pass. We parked the car and joined the tourists and pilgrims who'd come to see the 108 *chortens* spaced evenly over the hill. The mist was so dense that we could only see the *chortens* immediately around us and the outlines of those in the next circle. New *chortens* appeared as we walked, giving the impression of an endless field of religious relics.

One of the queens had this monument built in 2003 as a prayer for Bhutanese soldiers to return safe and victorious from their first battle in nearly a century. The United Liberation Front of Assam had made bases in southern Bhutan and were becoming a problem for the locals. The Indian army wanted to come in and clear out the guerillas, but the king knew that once the Indians were in the country they'd be there to stay. He was still trying to close the Indian army camps near our house which had been established decades before. The king decided that the Bhutanese army needed to take care of the problem with the ULFA themselves and he led them to war. The crown prince also joined the militia for the action.

Bhutanese people looked to the western world and saw our leaders sitting safely back in their offices while our troops went to war. They took great pride in their regents who led from the front line. The population moved to support this inexperienced army with prayer as it went to battle hardened guerillas. No one I spoke to about this ever recognised the irony of people with such respect for life praying for killings, but then the prayers may have been for minimal loss of life and it seems that was achieved. The Bhutanese army was so successful that the guerillas were crushed in a couple of days, with few casualties among the Bhutanese. The building of Dochu La was barely under way when the war was won.

After making our own prayers, we walked up to a *lakhang* – a small monastery – a few kilometres from the pass. The altitude was no longer causing me problems and my knee held up to the climb, but the walk back down was agony. I'd bought a trekking stick, but it wasn't enough. Every time I bent my left leg to lower my right foot, a knife cut through to the core of my knee.

'How can you be so weak?'

This was Dominique's way of dealing with her fear, though I didn't understand that at the time. She'd constantly tell herself that she was weak, or would fail the exam, so that if things went badly she wouldn't be disappointed. Usually she surprised herself with strength and success.

'I don't need your criticism, Dominique. I need your support. I need you to tell me I'll be okay.'

'But it's not okay. Look at you. You can hardly walk.'

'It's all in the mind. I just need to build up my confidence and I can't do that with you always telling me I'm a wreck.'

Dominique walked on in silence for a while, letting me limp on with my knives.

'You're right. I'm sorry. It's just that I hate to see you this way. But it's going to get better.'

I nodded my thanks.

'But maybe you should go home for a while. If you won't have an arthroscopy, at least let your father look at it.' My father was a successful chiropractor and even though Dominique had no faith in the profession, she knew I did. 'Besides, you haven't been home much in the last seven years and your parents won't be around forever. Go and spend some time with them and come back to me strong.'

'I'll think about it. Just let me get to the bottom of this hill first.'

'Do you think it was a black day?'

'A what?'

'You know. In the paper they list the days in the coming week and tell you if they're auspicious days or black days. Wednesday is a good day to get married or start a new venture. Don't go outside on Friday. Maybe the day you hurt your knee was a black day.'

'Who makes that up?'

'The monks.'

'You didn't used to believe in astrology.'

'No, but when you hear people talking about it every day as if it was real, you start to wonder.'

'They had a kick-off meeting for the showcase project the day I did this and you started *taikwondo,* so I doubt it was a black day.'

'It was just a thought. Besides, it got you to the bottom. We're here.'

Druk Air told me that I had to pay tourist rates for a ticket to Bangkok. At US$700, that was twice the price of the ticket from Bangkok to Sydney for half the flying time. Locals only paid the equivalent of about US$250. I couldn't see why I had to pay tourist rates when I wasn't a tourist. It would cost two months of Dominique's salary for both of us to go home at Christmas. Thankfully Yeshey offered to help me sort it out.

'The director of Druk Air is the father of one of my colleagues. I'll talk to him for you.' He picked up the phone.

I couldn't follow a word of the exchange, which was presumably all in Dzongkha. Most people also spoke Sharchop, a dialect from the East, Hindi from watching TV, and Nepali. With so many similar languages, I could never tell – a fact that didn't bode well for me ever learning one.

'He said that he can only offer local rates to expats with registered agencies,' Yeshey told me once he'd hung up. 'They just don't know about the French volunteers, that's all.'

'So how do we register?'

'You've got to have a letter from the Ministry of Agriculture, the invitation letter from the Ministry of Foreign Affairs as well as a request form from Druk Air.'

'That will take forever. Dominique's travelling this week and I don't know who to talk to at Agriculture.'

'I'll help. We'll work it out.'

Walking around town with Yeshey let me see just how small Thimphu was. Every ten paces he stopped to talk with an old friend, teacher or colleague. When we eventually made it to the Druk Air office, he looked at the queue and said, 'Let's go in the back. I know some people here.'

The only name I knew from the head office of the Ministry of Agriculture was Dr. Wangdi. Despite my reservations, I decided to ask for his help. Yeshey came with me, but stopped short of entering Dr. Wangdi's office. I would have welcomed his company, but he didn't know the history and it wasn't my place to tell him. Dominique had assured me that Dr. Wangdi kissing her wasn't harassment. He'd made a pass and failed and it was over. That didn't make me feel any better. I remembered how distraught she'd been when it happened, but I clenched my fists and took a few deep breaths before pushing the door open. Dr. Norbu was there as well. He sat back quietly while Dr. Wangdi treated me like an old friend he was delighted to see after so long. I forced myself to smile and speak calmly, when I really wanted to latch my teeth onto his throat. He promised to find the documents I needed, sure that there was even a copy of the invitation letter floating around.

I walked out before Dr. Wangdi could finish speaking.

'Please come any time and have a chat.'

I broke thirty for the first time on the drive home.

'I'm sure Ugyen will give you a lift.' Madeleine was another Australian who had arrived around the same time that I had. We were on our way home from dinner at one of Chris' friend's house. Our host had a couple of Australians staying and wanted to make a celebration of it. Since Dominique had taken the car on a business trip, I was stuck in town well after the taxi run had closed. I'd have to reserve one at night rates, which included paying for the trip back into town. Or Madeleine's friend could take me.

She'd been to Bhutan before and knew some important people. On this return trip, she was staying with a relative of the royal family and she was volunteering on behalf of one of her hosts. As it turned out, Ugyen had been playing pool with a friend who drove taxis and they came together to pick Madeleine up in a four-wheel-drive and were delighted to give me a lift.

'Thish is my friend Dooorji,' said Ugyen from the passenger seat. Madeleine and I were in the back. 'He'sh not ash jrunk ash I am.'

'Hi Murray. Nice to meet you. Where do you live?'

'In Babesa, but if you can drop me at the taxi stand, I'll be fine.'

'Don't be silly. I can take you home. How long have you been in Bhutan?'

We stopped at the police checkpoint, but as soon as they saw Ugyen, the policemen saluted and waved us through.

Dorji turned in his seat to see me properly. 'So what do you think of Bhutan?' The car drifted towards the cliff wall beside us as his hands dragged the wheel with him.

We were approaching the first corner fast and I pointed ahead, eyes wide and voice lost in fear.

'Don't worry,' said Dorji, turning back and hauling the car around the corner before turning to me again.

I was so scared, I began laughing. I was certain I would die on this trip, but somehow it seemed more important not to be rude than to worry about falling into the valley below. I'd had a good life. I just wanted to go quickly.

'Hey, Madeladeleine. Look what we fffound tsoday.' I heard the rustling of a cloth followed by a husky squeal.

'What is that?' Madeleine was laughing even harder than me. I wondered if she was expecting to die too. 'A boar?'

'Yepp. A boby bear. A baby boar.' I heard another rustle as he set the cloth back into place and the squealing stopped, but then he changed his mind. 'Here, you wanna hold it?'

Dorji slapped at his hands and the boar was put away again. We'd navigated four more corners despite the fact that Dorji spent most of his time looking backwards.

I was sure he was going to miss the fifth and let out an involuntary grunt of fear.

'What'sh ong? Are you shcared? Don' worry. If we have an acshiden, I'll jush go to the poleesh shtation tomorrow and shay I wash there, I wash driving and I wash jrunk. They won shay anything.'

Yeshey had spent an hour each day for the last week helping me gather the required documents. It took less than ten minutes for the Druk Air director to decide not to give us the local rates. I was furious. Dominique, now back from her trip, tried to calm me down.

'It's okay. We'll deal with it.'

'It's not okay. They take everything they can get from us, but won't help us when we need it. I'm helping on this showcase project out of generosity. Anna paid for the database herself, as useless as it was. We're pumping knowledge and money into this economy and they still want to charge us exorbitant fares to go home for a holiday. We've got good friends here. I'll write a letter and get them to sign it.'

'Murray, sshhhh. It's not that easy. The authorities will just tell you to leave if you don't like it. Lots of people want to work in Bhutan, or at least the government believes that. They wouldn't miss you.'

'We can at least make this a bit more public. Why would anyone want to work here when the government thinks it's their right to receive aid from foreigners and shows no appreciation. Just the opposite. They see us as another source of money to drain.'

'Don't. Keep talking like that and they won't only be happy to see you go, they'll kick you out like the English couple.'

'What English couple?'

'The ones in Phuentsholing. There was some petition against the government by the Southern Bhutanese in 1990. I don't know much about it, but some friends of this English couple asked them to proof-read the pamphlet. Their names appeared in the acknowledgements when it was printed and they were sent home immediately.'

'There's got to be something we can do.'

'No. If you get sent home, they'll send me home too and that will be the end of my career. Just leave it.'

It turned out that the hospital already had a couple of video-conferencing systems. They'd been sitting in storage since they were bought three years before. The original purpose had been the same as ours, so they were happy to let me configure them for our demonstration. One unit was dead out of the box, so I connected the other up to an ECG unit and arranged for the image to appear in high resolution on a computer on the same network. It took a couple of days to get it all working, but I was happy that the image was almost as clear as the original. A sweeping scan on the screen showed a pulsating blob that I assumed was a heart.

I called a nurse over, had her hook up a patient then took her to the transmitted image.

'Is that clear enough to be useful to you?'

'Yeah, I guess.' She pointed to some data in the top right corner. 'I usually just look at this number here.'

Dominique went silent when she realised it was me on the phone. I'd been back in Australia for three weeks.

'I just read your email. Dominique, what's going on?'

'Nothing.'

'It's not nothing. You tell me now, after we've been married for three months, that we're not really married. You had to wait until I was back in Australia, thousands of miles away, to tell me that it's all some kind of test.'

'That's not what I said, Murray. You're taking it all the wrong way.'

'How should I take it?'

'We had no choice but to get married. We did it to stay together. I don't know if it's going to work or not, but we had to try. You knew all that when we decided to marry.'

'That's not how I understood it at all. I had to make a quick decision and I decided that you were the one for me. Now you tell me that you're having more fun without me and that the test is over?'

'I didn't say that. When your knee is better, you can come back and join in our hikes and sport.'

'And if it takes me a while to recover properly?'

In the silence, I imagined I could hear a tear falling down her cheek.

'Is it worth me coming back at all?'

'I don't know.'

Sangay Wangchuk shared his office with Chris, so there was a picture of Jim Craig's shack alongside the king's portrait. The Australian icon made me long for the country I'd left eight years before.

'Is Chris a hard worker?' I asked him. 'Some people say that Australians are lazy.'

Sangay blew out through lips red from *doma*. 'That man is a machine. He wears so many hats that I don't know how he manages to do anything at all, but he does the work of five people.'

I held back a chuckle. Chris had previously told me that he'd never had so little to do.

'We thought you might not be coming back,' said Sangay, 'but it's good you did.'

I didn't know where to look. It had been a close thing. 'So, tell me about the showcase. Did the video-conferencing impress them?'

'I think so, but they were more impressed by the digital camera. We set up Photoshop so that they could print out a photo of themselves in front of the Eiffel Tower or the Pyramids.'

His shoulders bounced slightly as he laughed, eerily reminiscent of Dr. Norbu. 'They were like little kids.'

The group secretary arrived bringing two cups of *suja*, a spiced Himalayan drink made with salty butter. Dominique and the other Europeans often joked that the only way to drink it was to pretend it was soup.

'That would have been fun to see. Was the king there?'

'No. He reviews some of their main decisions, but mostly lets the government do its job. And if they decide to give us more money, I don't think he'll change that decision. I think we'll get it.'

'Does that mean more projects?'

'Not at the moment. We're too busy as it is.'

'Oh. Do you have any more work that I can help with?'

He thought for a few seconds. 'Nothing right now. Are you getting bored being a house husband?'

Words tumbled out, beyond my control. 'I'm not bored. I'm busy with writing and learning PHP and MySQL and using them to design web sites. It's just that I feel like I'm missing the experience of living in Bhutan. Everywhere else I've lived, I've worked with local people every day. Here, I get to hear all the stories about Bhutanese culture from Dominique, but it's all second-hand. When I was working with your team, I felt like I was part of the world again. I really enjoyed learning about your culture for myself.'

He smiled red. 'Send me your resumé and I'll pass it around. I'm sure someone will need your help.'

We continued chatting for half an hour while I finished my tea. Dominique would be proud. She couldn't make it through a whole cup yet.

I sensed hesitation in Dominique's silence as she approached my desk. I looked up, willing her to speak.

'Is it OK with you if I have some colleagues over for dinner on Saturday night?'

Was that all? 'Sure. As long as I'm allowed to be here, too. Do you want me to cook cheap Thai again?' I'd found that coconut milk gave rice and veggies a new flavour.

'No. I'm going to have a go at making crepes. I want to try that flour we got at the market last week and I'll use some of the local cheese we're trying to sell.' The Department of Livestock had urged farmers in Phobjika to increase cheese production and suddenly found themselves overstocked.

'Even better. How many are you expecting?'

'I have no idea. Maybe none. When I invited some of them today, they asked, "Is it compulsory?"'

Dominique put down her work things and came up behind me as I sat coding a finance tracking system. She wrapped her arms around my neck and kissed my temple.

I reached up to grab her arms, basking in her affection. '*Coucou.* How was work?'

'It was okay, except that they sprang another team meeting on me.' She straightened up and raised the pitch of her voice as she continued, 'Oh, didn't you know?'

'Who said that?'

'Everyone at the office says that whenever they forget to tell me something. Then they laugh.'

I took her hand. 'Don't be too hard on them. They've probably been talking about it for a while and just forgot that you don't speak Dzongkha. I'd take that as a compliment.'

Dominique puffed out her cheeks. 'Anna would have understood their discussions and known there was a meeting.'

I didn't want to talk about Anna. 'So, how was the meeting?'

'Two hours of sitting listening to Dzongkha when I could have been working. What about you? How was your day'

'Pretty good. I'm starting to get the hang of PHP.'

She pulled her hand out of mine. 'What is that smell?'

'Paprika's eating a rat under my chair. I guess he's showing off his kill. Can't you hear the bones crunching?'

Selden's brother, Pemba, let me limp into the police station alone. He was back in Bhutan after finishing university and had been kind enough to accompany me when I borrowed Kinga's car to make this urgent trip to town.

Dominique jumped up as soon as she saw me and tried to stifle her tears. 'Thanks, Sonam.'

The girl who'd been comforting her went to stand outside with others I'd seen in *taikwondo* gear.

'What happened?' I hadn't been able to make out much on the phone – just that she was at the police station and needed me.

'A group of kids came in to watch us practise and when they left, my bag was gone. I had everything in it – car keys, mobile phone, driver's licence, French national identity card, the watch Mum gave me for Christmas, everything. I thought it would be safe there. Bhutan is meant to be safe!'

Yeshey's brother was on duty and came over to see if he could help, looking very embarrassed. 'The sergeant will see you when he's free,' he said when it was clear there was nothing else he could offer.

While we waited, I scanned the binders on a bookcase across from us. Rape. Incest. Domestic violence. Larceny. Molestation. Murder. Each crime had at least one folder per year, dating back five years or more. Peace, it seemed, was an illusion.

'I'm sorry this had to happen to you,' said the sergeant when we were eventually ushered into his office. 'We don't get many foreigners in here at all and try to keep it that way. We don't want you getting a bad impression of our country.' He looked down at Dominique's statement. 'It says here you're working at the Ministry of Agriculture, madam. And you, sir?'

'I'm here with Dominique, but I'm helping a bit at DIT.'

The sergeant's stern expression softened. 'You work in IT? Perhaps you can tell me what this is.' He placed a hard drive on the table. 'I thought it might be,' he said when I'd told him. 'We found five of these on a seven-year-old kid earlier tonight.'

'Do you get a lot of theft cases, then?'

'See for yourself.' He nodded to the wall behind the door. It was covered in photographs. 'They're the culprits we've found in the last year.'

I scanned the photos while the sergeant took Dominique through her statement. The Bhutanese mugshots looked much like passport photos in size and format and they covered a whole wall. I looked closer. They were mostly children.

Five colleagues and a spouse turned up to Dominique's dinner party. It was good to see her enjoying herself with them. I ended up in a conversation with the spouse, neither of us knowing anyone else besides our partners.

'It's not that easy for Southern Bhutanese like us.' He kept his voice low and I was happy to indulge him by talking in whispers.

'What exactly does "Southern Bhutanese" mean?'

He looked surprised at my question and I realised I should have made efforts to understand this concept earlier. 'In the last century, Nepalis were invited to Bhutan to help build the *dzongs* and roads. They were allowed to stay when the work was finished.'

'Do you still consider yourselves Nepali, then?'

'That's the whole thing. I consider myself Bhutanese, but I can't have citizenship, even though my parents and grandparents were born here.'

'What country are you a citizen of then? Nepal?'

'No. I don't have citizenship anywhere. And I'm just a resident here, like you. I can work and travel more easily, but I'd never be able to get a decent job in the government.'

'But that's...!' I looked at the group on the other side of the room. There was a mixture of Bhutanese and Nepalis chatting happily. 'It's hard to believe that anyone here could be racist. Everyone's so friendly.'

'It's more like nationalism or culturalism than racism.'

'So I guess you don't keep a picture of the king on your wall at home.'

'We do. The king's an amazing man who has done so much to improve this country.' He was looking directly at me, but I got the feeling he was fighting the urge to look around to see if anyone was listening in. 'But you know, we're Christians and that's not allowed here. We have to pretend to be Buddhist with our Bhutanese friends.'

'Huh? How did you become Christian?'

'Lots of Nepali people are,' he said. 'I'm not sure how it started. It came in through India, I guess.'

I recalled a comment from a conversation I'd had early in my stay that I didn't understand. 'I heard that there was some problem with Southern Bhutanese in 1990. What was that about?'

This time, he did look around. 'This isn't a good time to talk about that.' He looked relieved when Dominique approached.

She smiled at him before turning to me. 'Can you help me with the crepes, Murray?'

Dominique thrust my coat at me and playfully dragged me to the car to drive a few of her colleagues home after the dinner. Summer was approaching and even at midnight it was warm enough that I didn't need the coat. I'd originally stayed back to wash up while she drove them, but she'd been stopped at a police check. She had a letter from the police sergeant to say that her licence had been stolen, but that wasn't enough. They wanted papers from the RSTA itself, which she couldn't get until Monday. It was only through the intervention of her colleagues that she'd been allowed to drive back to get me. The police had wanted her to leave the car with them, even though that meant four people walking many kilometres along a cliff-top in the middle of the night.

I kept the car to twenty, to the amusement of my passengers. The height still made me uncomfortable and I wasn't used to driving these winding roads in the dark.

We rounded a corner and found the police standing in the road, waiting for the few cars still braving the darkness. I wound down my window as I pulled up, but the policeman waved me through after a glance.

'What?' Dominique shouted. 'How come they let you go without a check?'

'Probably because I drive better than you.'

'Rubbish. At this speed, you're a menace to traffic. It's because you're a man.'

'It might just be because you'd already told them I had a licence.'

'And why should they believe that? Anyway, they never check you, but they check me every time. They even pass my licence to their superior for checking while they chat to me. They never care that I'm in a hurry.'

'They're probably lonely. They've been standing around all day on their own and you've got a friendly face.'

'So do you, but they don't stop you. They just stop the girls. It's sexual harassment.'

I put down my plate of *ema datshi* and sat back, content. Dominique had stayed with Selden on a recent training week in Paro and learnt to make the national dish. It wasn't perfect, but it was good enough to give us a break from the days of rice and veggies and I knew Dominique would get better at it.

'I don't follow you,' I said. 'How can a couple of big houses or expensive flats ruin life for the Bhutanese? They'll never be the ones renting them anyway.'

'They don't have to be. Even if they're built for expats, it changes the market dynamics. There's less space for housing that's affordable to the locals.'

Paprika, seeing that we'd finished eating, jumped onto Dominique's lap and purred loudly.

'How many rats have you eaten today?' she said. 'I hope you cleaned yourself. At least it's a lot quieter now, without all the scratching in the walls.'

'There's plenty of space,' I said, bringing the conversation back to economics. 'And look at all the construction that's going on now. With so many new places, the prices can't be high.'

'But look at how fast the population of Thimphu is growing. Anna said that it doubled in size in the time she was here and we've seen it grow in just the last six months. And still there's no shortage of people wanting homes.'

'Fine, but they're not renting the big places. The prices of expat accommodation might be high, but if the locals can't afford higher prices, why would the low-end market change?'

Paprika extended a clawed foot and I swatted it away.

'Because the developers will see that they can get better money from building expat-style homes, so they'll all start doing it. There won't be much left that the locals can afford.'

There was a gap in the logic as far as I could see, but Dominique was the economist. It would bear thinking about further, especially in relation to the kids that begged me for money on my way home every day. I was sure that only started because rich tourists handed out coins. Was that where youth crime began too?

I lifted Paprika off Dominique's lap, gritting my teeth at the wails. I worried that the cat was psychologically damaged. Were cats always so needy? Did they normally sound like a spoilt child? Putting Paprika out of my mind, I pulled Dominique up after me. 'Come on. We should take advantage of the longer days. Let's go and have a look at the rice paddies. The stalks are starting to come up. You can keep trying to explain while we walk.'

Tshering Wangchuk led me into the Royal Institute of Management computer lab and called to the class to pay attention. Thirty boys and girls in matching *ghos* and *kiras*, sitting paired in front of computers, turned to listen to their teacher.

'This is Murray. He's an expert in PHP and MySQL and he's volunteered to help you with your study.' He turned to me. 'Murray, why don't you introduce yourself.'

I assured them that I was no expert, but even with only a couple of months' practice, I'd been able to put together a couple of web-based applications, one of which was the finance tracking system. These were easy technologies to learn and they were free – the perfect tools for a developing economy.

The students returned to their computers as soon as I finished.

'Don't worry about not being a real expert,' Tshering said. 'Our level is really low.'

When I heard Tshering talk that way, it occurred to me that neither of us were inspiring confidence in the students. 'I'm sure you're just being modest. What have you done with PHP so far?'

'Nothing really. Oh, there's the RIM web page, but I just cut and paste bits from other sites, then change the pictures or fonts to make it ours. I've never coded anything original myself.'

'Well, who puts together the lesson plans, then?'

'We don't have lesson plans. We downloaded the labs from a university in Switzerland and the students go through them at their own pace. That's why we were so glad when DIT said you wanted to help. Now, I've got other things to do. You don't have to stay here, either. If they need you, they'll find you at your desk.'

I chose to stay and made a lap of the class, looking over shoulders to see what each group was working on. Everyone was working at their own pace so they were all doing different exercises. All the exercises at this early stage asked them to create simple programs as a way of teaching the structure of the programming language.

'Sir, sir.' A boy called me over. 'Sir, this isn't working.'

'Why not?'

'But sir is the teacher. If you don't know...'

I squatted down beside him and his partner. 'Hang on. I'm not here to give you the answers, just to help you figure it out for yourself. I don't even know what you're trying to do, yet.'

A boy from the group beside them had brought a chair from somewhere else in the room and directed me to sit properly.

'Thanks. Now, what do you expect to happen?'

A four-wheel-drive pulled up beside me as I walked to work and I looked up to see who might offer me a lift.

'Hi Murray.' It was Tshering Tashi, the founder of the Australia Bhutan Friendship Association, a friendly young man from a wealthy family. 'How's things?'

He gave those two words a tone of such genuine interest that I found myself telling him all our concerns, including Dominique's problems with Dr. Wangdi. He pulled the car to the side of the road and switched off the engine.

'Do you know about RENEW?'

I admitted that I didn't.

'It stands for 'Respect, Educate, Nurture and Empower Women'. They deal with all sorts of sexual discrimination and women-specific issues. It's sponsored by Ashi Sangay Choden Wangchuk.'

'That's one of the queens, right?'

'Right. You should talk to them, or get Dominique to. I'm sure they'll be able to help.'

'Dominique will be worried that it will make her job harder if her bosses and colleagues know that she reported it.'

'I'm sure that RENEW will find a discreet way to handle it and Dominique can remain anonymous.'

'What about the fact that she's a foreigner?'

'That won't matter. If this man would harass her, he'd harass a Bhutanese woman too. It needs to be dealt with.'

'I'm not sure that she'll want to do it, but I'll let her know.'

He wrote a number on a scrap of paper. 'Here. It's up to her, but we want to stop problems like this early. I hope she'll report it.'

We said our goodbyes and I watched Tshering Tashi drive off, feeling happier than I had in a while. Sure, Bhutan had problems, but they were dealing with them. And Dominique had support if she chose to use it.

'Murray, the director wants to meet you and there's a meeting about something to do with Australia on now. Can you join us?'

I followed Kuenga, the head of RIM's IT department, to the other corner of the university building. He barged into the office and gestured for me to take a seat at one of two bench sofas flanking a coffee table. I chose the seat closest to the corner of the room and watched as the director finished a phone call. He was a solid man with thinning black hair. As soon as he put the phone down, he bellowed for someone called Ugyen and headed over to sit opposite me. Kuenga had taken the seat to my left.

Ugyen poked his head in the door and accepted an order for six teas, then disappeared to be replaced by three other members of staff.

'You must be Mr. Murray.' The director introduced the other members of the team and made much of the fact that I was helping RIM out of the goodness of my heart. 'Now, we've been invited to participate in a twinning relationship with the University of New England in Australia.'

'What's twinning?' I suddenly realised that I'd interrupted and added the honorific 'la' to reduce the insult.

The director turned to me with no sign of irritation at being interrupted. 'Twinning is when a course is offered by two universities together. Students in Bhutan could take a course at RIM, but be awarded a degree from UNE.'

The relationship made sense. Some of my Bhutanese friends had studied at UNE. I nodded and he continued. While he talked, I watched the other staff and noticed that they all kept their eyes on his chest. Apparently it was impolite to make eye contact with your superiors in Bhutan. I tried to copy them, but found that looking into people's eyes was a difficult habit to break.

The director didn't seem to mind. In fact, he directed most of his comments at me and I wondered if he found the eye contact refreshing. How could he tell if the others were listening when he couldn't see their eyes?

Tea arrived and the discussion continued around me, but with the director looking mostly at me I felt that I was the focus of attention. Unsure what I was there for, I listened to everything, but understood little. These men were all better educated than I was. Instead, my thoughts turned to the tea, still sitting on the table in untouched cups before each person. The staff were probably all waiting for the director before taking theirs. Or perhaps they'd already had ten cups that day and were hoping they wouldn't have to drink any more.

'Can you help us, Mr. Murray?'

The discussion had wound down and I'd contributed nothing besides nods. 'I'm not sure. I've never done a master's degree. I know that an undergraduate degree is primarily about teaching students to learn, but I haven't the slightest idea of what a master's degree is really about. But if there's anything I can do, I'm happy to help.'

The director looked disappointed and, suddenly in need of a distraction, I reached for my tea.

'Oh, sorry.' The director picked up his cup and just got a sip in before I broke protocol. 'Please, go ahead.'

Our path broke free of the forest cover on a small plateau marked by a prayer wheel. From there, we could look out across the valley to a four-hundred-metre-high cliff, sheer but for an invisible ledge built just over halfway up. A temple clung impossibly to that ledge, far more spectacular than any photo could portray. This was Taktsang, the most revered of *lakhangs*, said to be where Guru Rimpoche first landed in Bhutan when he flew in on the back of a tigress.

Michael and May, a newly arrived Kiwi couple, had organised this weekend away to make the trek up the cliff. Dominique led us in walking the prayer wheel through three circuits. A rod protruding from the top of the wheel struck a bell with each circuit, adding texture to the view. Nearby, a tall stand of prayer flags fluttered in the breeze, the wind carrying the prayers to the gods.

I found the Bhutanese propensity to automate prayer amusing. At some temples, locals went to great efforts to direct streams to turn prayer wheels in the manner of mills, just so the prayers painted on the wheel would continue unmanned until the river stopped flowing.

We were still standing mesmerised when a Bhutanese family reached the clearing. They had two teenage girls dressed in Stussy gear with glossy lips and mascara.

'Oh look, Mum,' said the older one. 'It's gorgeous, just like I remember.'

We began talking with the family. The father, Tashi, worked in construction and was obviously doing well enough to send his daughters to school in the US. They were delighted to walk with us to show off their monument and to make sure we didn't lose the path.

'That's it there.' The mother pointed to a ledge on the cliff a few hundred metres above us and still off in the distance. 'You can see the cairn straight ahead. From there it drops back down to the right and in to the waterfall, then back up to the *lakhang*. Come on. Before the day gets too hot.'

Tashi asked what we all did in Bhutan. Michael was also a house husband, looking after May who had come out to finish off a project to base the government compensation and promotions systems on performance.

'You're from New Zealand?' asked Tashi. 'I know a man from New Zealand. A horrible man. He comes out here and thinks he can change all the rules, but he doesn't know how it works here. We can't do things the same way as you do them in developed countries.'

We knew he was talking about Arnold, a gentle man who'd been asked to come to Bhutan to help make the construction industry safer. He was continually frustrated by the locals who made excuses for the poor conditions and materials, but understood that all he could do was point out problems and suggest improvements. The company building a bridge for the new highway running along the valley floor, he'd told us, was already two years behind schedule. Now the construction company complained that first-grade concrete was too expensive, so they were going to use second-grade material. That was one mistake he'd managed to stop.

'He comes in here and tells us how to do our jobs, but he doesn't know anything. He should just go back to his own country and make rules there.'

We could have told him that any new rules were made by the Bhutanese government based on good advice, but this wasn't our fight. Instead we made soothing sounds and non-committal acknowledgements of his frustration. Then suddenly we arrived at the cairn and looked down on the white walls of the *lakhang*. Freshly washed red robes were spread out to dry on the red-brown roofs. A couple of young monks tussled in the courtyard, a waist-high wall protecting them from a fall to an early reincarnation.

The steps to the waterfall felt too narrow for the drop and I hugged the cliff on the descent, realising it would be months before my knee was back at full strength. From there, we climbed up a broad rock staircase to present our papers to the guard.

The *lakhang* seemed to climb up the cliff from temple to temple. Guru Rimpoche had slept in a cave at the lowest level. At the highest was a two-storey temple. Dominique, Michael and May all headed up to the top level while I stayed to make obeisance at the ground floor, where a six-year-old monk watched my every move.

I pondered the relative merits of starting children on this path so young, whether they made the choice themselves or not. They must lose most of the carefree spirit of their childhood, but it should expose them to ideas of tolerance at an impressionable age.

Along with Tashi, I pressed my palms together at chest height, then again with my thumbs touching my forehead before prostrating myself in front of the altar. I did this three times in accordance with tradition, then folded a ten-ngultrum note, prayed over it and presented it as a donation at the altar.

The monk held out the jug of holy water and I followed Tashi in cupping my hands to receive a splash that I would use to cleanse my body inside and out – with a sip and a wipe over my head. He held the jug up, but stopped short of pouring, instead muttering something to Tashi.

'He wants to know if you're Buddhist.'

'No, I'm not,' I said, choosing to be honest, 'but I respect the customs and would like to learn more.'

I waited while the two exchanged a few more words.

'He says you'll have to leave.'

'Sir.' A pretty girl stood before my desk, a shy smile below eyes that wouldn't meet mine. 'I can't make it work. Please help me, sir.'

I glanced at the clock on the wall behind Kuenga, who was playing solitaire. The lesson had started and I should have been in there anyway.

I directed her to lead the way and followed her through to the outer staff room where Tshering, Wangdi and the other male staff were clustered around a desk making appreciative noises over something on the screen.

'Tshering, are you going to teach the class?'

'No. I've got things to do.'

I glanced at the girl – I thought her name was Deki Wangmo – patiently waiting in the doorway, wondering how far to push this in her presence. To Tshering I said, 'I'm only meant to be helping you teach, you know, not doing everything for you.'

'I'm busy, I told you. I've got to do the university newsletter and I need to edit video for a friend. You know more than me about PHP anyway.'

Deki shrugged her shoulders at me.

I told her that I'd be with her in a minute and went over to see what they were looking at. It was a video under the banner 'Latin Babes Love Big Black Dicks.'

'Men,' Dominique muttered. 'You're all the same.'

I'd had to follow her into the bedroom again. From the way she was fumbling with the brooch on her *tego*, she would burst into tears at any moment.

I made my voice as gentle as I could. 'Tell me what happened.'

'I told you I'd found someone else I could work with, didn't I? I can't be close to Dr. Wangdi and Dr. Norbu is useless, so I've been working with Wangchuk from marketing.'

She gave up on the brooch and dropped onto the edge of the bed, still refusing to look at me.

'It was just like before. As soon as we started working well together, he tried to kiss me.' She looked up with fire in her eyes. 'Why do you men always think that if a girl is happy to be with you that she wants sex?'

'Not all men are like that, Dominique.'

'Oh, so it's only with me then. Why is my *karma* so bad? What did I do in a past life to always get the perverts?'

'It's not *karma*, Dominique. You don't even believe in *karma*. It's just bad luck.'

'I don't know any more. My mother's given me three watches and they've all been stolen. Every time I work overseas, some man thinks I'm his sex slave. That's more than just bad luck.'

I sat down beside her and let her fall into my arms. 'Do you want to talk to RENEW now?'

'No,' she said, the fire returning to her eyes. 'I stood up to him. I told him that I was happy to work with him, but that's all it was. I told him I have a husband.'

A small thrill ran through me at the word husband. After five months, she was finally thinking of me that way.

'Good for you. What did he say to that?'

'He said, "That's okay. Just tell me when you're ready."'

'Sir, sir. What's wrong with this?'

I took Deki Wangmo through the usual process. What was she trying to do? What did she expect to happen? What was happening instead? Why might that be?

'I don't know, sir.'

'Of course you do.'

The girl dropped her head and I made an effort to control myself. Snapping at the students wouldn't help. It would just make them scared to ask questions.

'Remember what I told you yesterday about text strings?' And the day before. And the day before that. And before that when I gave a lesson on the topic. 'It was a different exercise, but the concept is exactly the same.'

I opened a new window and demonstrated the principle, then watched her apply it to her own problem.

'Right. Now, remember that when you get a strange result tomorrow.'

I went back to my desk at the end of the lesson and raised my concerns with Kuenga.

'They don't seem to be learning anything. The same people make the same mistakes and ask the same questions every day.'

'I hope you don't just fix their problem.'

'No.' Dominique had taught me well.

'Good. The Japanese volunteer we had before you would do everything for them. They don't learn that way.'

At least the department head understood. Give a man a fish and he'll eat for a day. Teach a man to fish and he'll feed himself for life. These kids needed to learn, but more than that, they needed to learn how to learn. And they needed to break problems down so they could find the real cause. I didn't know if that ability was being developed at RIM.

'How's Tshering Wangchuk doing?' asked Kuenga.

'I have no idea. He never goes to the class and never has the time to talk about it.'

'Tell him he has to. I know you won't be here forever and he needs to run this class himself when you leave. It's his job to get as much knowledge as he can from you in that time.'

And that was the real goal in aid work. Teach the fisherman to teach others and whole villages could feed themselves.

I stepped out of the Indian army canteen and headed home with a bag of *samosa* and *pakoras* for dinner. The Indian snacks cost about five cents each and were the perfect accompaniment to salad now that the weather was getting warmer. That day at RIM had been a good one, with some of the students asking new questions. I'd even had to go away and do some research in the lunch break so I could give a short lesson in the afternoon on an unfamiliar topic.

One of the stray dogs detached itself from the pack and came over to walk beside me, wagging its whole body.

'Hey, girl.' I reached down to pat her. 'You're the only friendly one. You must have been born into a home. Why can't you teach your friends to be nice?'

She nuzzled the hem of my *gho* and walked to heel when I started moving again. We came upon another gang of dogs closer to home. They jumped up and started barking and growling at my friend, but wouldn't come near her while a person was there. They'd been kicked too many times.

'Hello. Where are you going?' This kid, or one of his friends, asked me the same question whenever he saw me walking home. It was usually accompanied by the mimed action of screwing in a light bulb.

I knew it was going to become annoying one day, but for now it didn't hurt to be friendly and to give them a chance to practise their English with a native speaker.

'I'm going home.'

'Where do you live?'

I pointed to the roof up the hill in the orchard. 'I live in that house.'

The urchin held out his hand. 'Give me ten rupee.'

The computer lab was empty when I arrived. I waited ten minutes before going to see Tshering Wangchuk.

'There's a soccer game on today, so there'll be no class.'

'Why didn't you tell me?'

'Oh! Didn't you know?'

They were the same words that so frustrated Dominique. Now I began to understand how she felt. 'No. How could I?'

'It's been planned for a week.'

'And you probably all talked about it in Dzongkha. Bugger. I could have stayed at home. Okay. I'm here now and we need to talk about the class. I spoke to Kuenga and he said that he wants you to learn everything I know about PHP, but you need to join me in the class.'

'You can just tell me afterwards.'

'How will you learn it that way? The students don't learn it even when I show them five times.'

'Oh, don't bother with that. It takes too long. Just fix any problems for them.'

'Come on, Murray,' said Tshering Wangchuk. 'Wangdi's shouting lunch today.'

Wangdi was the network teacher, quieter and more capable than Tshering, but I had little contact with him. I followed the group out of the room and through the main doors, but instead of turning right to the canteen, we turned left.

'Where are we going?'

'To Wangdi's house, I told you. He's providing lunch.'

The house was a cottage on campus, next to the students' quarters. Wangdi's father was in the front yard, sitting on the low stone wall and painting a cabinet. From the red base and intricate detail in vibrant colours around the joins, I recognised it as an altar for a home. A devout family, then, or too poor to have one made for them.

Wangdi's wife met us at the door and directed us to the living room. In the gloom, dots on the walls looked like mould, but as we entered, they stirred and zoomed around us. Summer was almost in full swing and the rains hadn't come. It was perfect weather for flies.

Slowly the room began to fill up and I met a number of faculty members I'd never seen before I managed to catch our host.

'Wangdi, no one's told me why you're doing this. Is it a celebration?'

'Yes.' Pride filled his voice and his submissive hunch was gone. 'I'm celebrating an increase in my *karma*. Excuse me. I have to greet the other guests.'

How could he be so sure of an increase in his *karma*? That was like saying that I'd had an improvement in my fate.

Food appeared in quantities disproportionate to the number of guests and to the apparent wealth of the family. Perhaps that was the clue. He must have found some money, got a raise or received a commendation from the king. I cornered Tshering and, not knowing if it was taboo to discuss, brought the conversation around to the cause.

'Do you know what scriptures are?' he asked.

'Yes. Holy documents.'

'Right. Well, there are many scriptures in Buddhism and it takes a long time to read them all, but the more you read, the greater your *karma*.'

'So Wangdi has been reading some of these scriptures then.' That didn't seem to be reason to celebrate on such a grand scale.

'Not just some. All of them. That takes weeks or even months and brings a huge benefit to *karma*. It might be enough to ensure he's reincarnated in a high position.'

'How long has he been doing this? I haven't seen him take any time off work.'

'He didn't read them himself. He paid a couple of monks to read them for him.'

We knocked on Mike's door, but it was May who opened it. Mike, one of the friends that Dominique had gone hiking with while I was back in Australia, was sitting on the other side of his living room, head hung low to hide a black eye.

Dominique ran to him. '*Putain!* Mike, what happened?'

He glanced up at her then at the ground again. 'Wait until everyone's here. I only want to say it once.'

May offered to get us a drink and Dominique joined her in the kitchen. I went to talk to Michael.

'Do you know anything about this?'

'Only that he's leaving the country tomorrow.'

'Oh.'

The room held a morbid silence until the door opened and Arnold, the construction safety expert, came in.

'Okay,' said Mike, reluctantly. 'I think that's everyone.'

We all sat down to hear the story.

'Roger and I had a few beers last night, watching the All Blacks win the rugby. Then I went into town to celebrate and had a few more.'

I probably wasn't the only one thinking that it sounded like Mike had brought whatever happened on himself – with his muscled physique and crew cut, he looked like a thug – but no one said a word. I knew Dominique, at least, saw him as a gentle bloke.

'On the way home, a dog started barking and came at me. I thought it was a stray dog. You know how they are at night.'

Living out of town, Dominique and I had little personal experience, but everyone who lived in town complained about the stray dogs hunting in packs once the light had gone.

'I chased this dog and it ran into someone's yard where they were having a party. A few of the men came down to see what was going on. When I realised it was their dog, I told them to keep the stupid thing chained up so it didn't harass people on the street.'

Here, we all nodded. We'd all wanted to do the same thing.

'They were big shots, which just made me angrier. We ended up in a shouting match. Then one of them started to move around behind me.'

He dropped his head again and wrung his hands. His head remained down when he continued.

'I was worried that they'd try to tackle me, so I swung at the bloke who was moving. The next thing I knew, I was on the ground being kicked by the whole group.

'I came back here and Roger helped clean me up a bit. He told me to let it be, but I didn't listen. I figured those bastards deserved to be taught a lesson, so I went and told the police what happened, but the big shots got there before me.

'The police told me the other side of the story – that it was me that started it.' His voice broke. 'I'd thought I was the victim, but it's true that I took the first swing. It was my fault.'

May broke the silence that ensued. 'But that's no reason to go home. You're doing good work here and you were enjoying it.'

Mike took a swig of beer and lowered his head again.

'They gave me a choice. They said I could leave immediately or I could go to gaol for six months.'

Three girls we'd met at Cheri Goempa during the morning had offered to share their picnic lunch with us. We walked back down the hill to a glade by the frothing turquoise river. Each girl put down their cloth-wrapped package and untied it to reveal interlocking insulated containers. I began salivating as soon as the covers were lifted on red rice, *ema datshi* and a couple of meat dishes that I didn't recognise.

'Are you all at school together?' Dominique asked. 'Or have you finished already?'

'We're doing computer college,' said one of the girls who had large eyes and full lips. 'None of us got the marks to continue at school.'

'What do you learn at college?' I asked.

She looked at my chest, then away, unable to meet my eyes. 'It's mostly bookkeeping.'

'How much longer do you have to go?' Dominique spoke this time, putting a hand on my knee. You're not a monster, it said, but leave the talking to me this time. The girls began smiling again.

'We're almost finished,' said the girl with the lips, clearly the most vocal of the group. 'Just a couple more months.'

'What then?'

One of the girls, more shapely than the others but with a too-thin nose, passed me a meat dish along with a container lid to use as a plate. I helped myself, noting the flicker of discomfort on Dominique's face. I hadn't had food poisoning yet and needed some meat in my diet, so I ignored her.

'We have to try to find a job in a private company,' said the last girl, whose intense green eyes still refused to meet mine.

'That's difficult for us.' The shapely girl passed Dominique the *ema datshi*. 'There aren't so many private companies in Thimphu and there are lots of people in our college.'

Dominique scooped a collection of chillies onto her lid-plate. 'What about the government?'

The spokesgirl didn't wait to finish her mouthful before speaking. 'You need to finish school and pass special exams to work at the government. I can't do that.' Her friends nodded at her words.

'There must be other options available to you. Can you study something else?'

'It takes money to study. If I can't get a job after this, I'll probably have to start my own business, but that takes money too.'

'What about sir?' one asked Dominique. 'What do you do?'

Dominique's fingers tightened on her spoon at being called 'sir,' but she responded politely. The rest of the conversation centred on Dominique's work.

'Please, have more.' The intense-eyed girl pushed the rice and her meat dish at me.

'I'll have a little more because it's so delicious, but I'm really full already.' Two plates stretched even me.

'Oh, you must. We can't take it home with us. It must all be eaten. And if you don't, we'll have to.'

The shapely girl laughed. 'And we're too fat already.'

Like girls from any country, they were too skinny to be complaining about their weight, but I wondered how they would have managed to finish it all with just three people, when it was too much for five. Had they known that they'd find someone to share it with?

Finally it was done and we packed up. Dominique helped them with the empty containers and I reached for the plastic bottles.

'Don't worry about them, sir.'

Dominique and I both looked up at the spokesgirl in astonishment.

'Why?'

'We won't use them again. Just leave them there.'

'It's because they haven't ever had plastic before,' Dominique said over the usual rice and veggies that night.

'What is?'

'Those girls today leaving their rubbish on the ground. Plastic is a new thing here. Until a few years ago they only ever had wood and paper, so they normally just threw their scraps in the river or left them to rot.'

Paprika watched the fork as I raised it from the plate to my mouth, more to pass the time before he was allowed on our laps than any desire for the vegetables, I thought. 'But surely they know it's a problem with plastic. Environment is one of the four pillars of Gross National Happiness. With global warming all over the news everywhere, they must realise.'

'I heard that the government tried to ban plastic bags. It was probably easier to do that than to teach the people what to do with them. They haven't had generations of technology like us, so they haven't had to deal with the problems yet. They still think they can go on living life as usual and just take the benefits.'

'Why didn't banning plastic bags work?' I recalled that our collection of plastic bags had enticed the landlady's mother to steal from us.

'From what I've heard, shopkeepers complained that paper bags broke too easily and refused to use them. I think the police gave up trying to force them.'

Three desks crowded the office of the visa section. While I waited for my turn, I reached behind to check that my *gho* was straight. It needed a little adjustment because I refused to wind the belt as tightly as the locals did, but otherwise it was pretty good. I thought I was getting the hang of it.

Sonam Wangdi, who had the desk by the window, waved me to a seat. She was the representative of the Chief of Protocol and the only one in this office that seemed to know the processes. Hers was a name worth remembering.

'Have you got everything?' she asked.

'I hope so.' I pushed the papers across the desk. This was my fourth visit, just to get a visa for my friend Dave. Dave had done a lot of running around getting the Australian documents that I needed to apply for marriage in France. When Dominique found out that she could invite three guests who would then be free of the US$200 per day fee, she immediately thought of Dave. If he ever got the visa, it would be the first time they met.

On the first visit, I'd come to pick up the visa application form and was told I'd also need a letter from Dominique's employer, the Ministry of Agriculture. That much was standard procedure for any request in Bhutan. The second time I'd come, an underling had told me that I needed to bring a copy of our passports and assured me that was all. The third time, it was a Personal Guest Application Form that was separate to the visa application. I was glad to see Sonam back and really hoped this time would be the last.

Sonam clicked her tongue as she perused the documents, placing each one firmly on her desk when she decided it was sufficient. As she removed the last page, surprise flickered over her broad features. Once more she went through the pile before looking up at me.

'Where's the letter to the Chief of Protocol?'

'It's here,' I said, pulling the Ministry letter from the stack.

'No. You need a personal letter from yourself to the Chief of Protocol to state that David will be your guest and that you'll take care of him.'

I wanted to throw it all in her face. I wanted to jump up and down. I wanted to scream. I settled for speaking through my teeth. 'Is that all? The letter from the Ministry, the visa application form, the letter to the Chief of Protocol, the copy of our passports and the Personal Guest Application Form? I'd hate to have to come again and take up your valuable time.'

'Yes, that's all.' She seemed oblivious to the sarcasm. 'Come back tomorrow and I'll make sure it's ready for next week.'

I got up, just restraining myself from sending the chair flying. As I brushed past one of the locals waiting his turn, he grabbed my arm.

'I'm a tour guide, so I go through this process a lot. You'll need three copies of the visa application form.'

It had taken the five of us most of the day to reach the ridge above Thimphu and I was keen to get down to our campsite quickly. I started down the dry riverbed while Dominique, Michael, May and Madeleine rested. The river stones underfoot made this one of the hardest parts of the trek, despite the gentleness of the slope. At four thousand metres, we were above the tree line, but scrub covered the surrounding hills. A stone rolled under my foot and my knee locked up, not for the first time on this descent. Panic still jolted every muscle, but not as severely.

There was no pain. Just shock. And fear. I took a deep breath, made sure my leg was aligned in front of me and bent it carefully until it clicked through the block. My father said it sounded like a meniscus tear – that the cartilage had been roughed up while I'd been walking around on a misaligned knee and now it was catching in the joint. But would the rough bits be smoothed out by walking or would they tear further? I chose to believe the former.

I could hear voices behind me, but I kept my attention on the rocks at my feet, choosing a sturdy looking position for my next step. When a break in the rocks appeared, I looked up. A pool of water ahead was more swamp than lake, but its banks would make as good a campsite as any. There was enough flat space for three tents near ruins of what might have been a small cottage or even a yak herder's hut. Low scrub covered the hills around us, except for the riverbed we'd walked down and a swarm of yak trails leading out the other side. A rock cairn covered a tiny island in the middle of the lake.

I was musing on who might have braved the cold waters to build it when Dominique stepped up beside me and took my hand.

'See, your knee's going to be fine.'

'Yep. I'll be ready to do the Snowman Trek with you soon.' It was known as one of the toughest treks in the world, taking twenty five days, much of which was above five thousand metres.

Dominique's pretty smile grew wider. 'Are you serious?'

'Yes. As long as we have horse support, I think I'll be able to do it.' Dorina, a woman Dominique had hiked with while I was in Australia, had the insane idea of trying to do the trek carrying everything on her back, but I thought we could talk her round.

'We can do the Snowman Trek together.' Dominique pulled me down into a kiss and for once, I didn't care that my knee locked up in the process.

May's voice sounded right behind me. 'Cut it out, you two.'

I looked up to see the rest of the group arrive. 'Come on,' I said to Dominique. 'Let's get the tent up.'

But by the time we'd made camp, I had a headache and knew that altitude was going to be as much a problem as my knee for the big trek.

Dominique and I had left the others to take their time and camped on our own the second night. Dominique wanted to get back early so she could do some preparation for the week ahead. I was beginning the final, long descent when I came across a stout Russian man carrying a small day pack and supporting himself with a walking staff.

'How much further is it?' he asked, puffing each word.

'That depends on where you're camping. You should ask your guide.'

'Oh, he's terrible,' said a woman behind him. 'He's such a slave driver, always demanding we walk faster. This is meant to be a holiday, but he treats it like a fitness camp.'

The Druk Path was known as the easiest trek available for tourists in Bhutan. If they were having trouble here, perhaps they should have stayed in their hotel. But then, they would probably have whined that the towels weren't soft enough. Bhutan charged an enormous daily minimum for tourists and ended up with this kind of visitor, while those that would appreciate the Bhutanese environment couldn't afford to come here.

I pushed past them and headed further down the path until I met a man in a *gho* coming up.

'Where is your guide?' he asked me.

'I'm the guide.' I loved giving this line, almost as much as I loved telling people I was a house husband. The confusion it caused was always worth a laugh. 'We live in Bhutan.'

'We?'

'My wife and I. She's still behind me. She's not so good on the uphills, but she'll catch me up now we're going down.'

'I won't just catch you up. I'll pass you.' Dominique seemed to be skipping down the hill, bouncing off rocks and trees like a character in a Chinese action movie, joy in every step.

'Wow. You're married to a mountain goat. And you're even carrying your own packs. I wish my customers were like you.'

'Was that them I just passed?'

'Yes, but there are more behind.' He gave me a look that combined frustration and exhaustion. 'We're meant to be at the campsite by now, but we're only halfway.'

I looked down and saw a huge American woman riding a small horse up the hill.

'Phew, I didn't realise this would be such hard work,' she said as she approached.

I looked at the poor horse and thought I saw it roll its eyes.

Dominique came out while I was introducing Dave to the dog. I left him to get acquainted and went to stand with her.

'You're wearing lipstick and mascara. What's the occasion?'

She lowered her eyes. 'I want your friends to like me.'

Dave left the dog when he saw Dominique and hurried over. '*Bonjour* Dominique. *Enchanté.*'

'*Enchanté en rencontre.*'

Dave looked at me, his incomprehension clear.

'I think she said that she's happy to meet you too.'

They looked at each other awkwardly for a few seconds, then Dominique stepped up and greeted him the French way, with three kisses on alternate cheeks.

'Come inside. I got some *samosa* for lunch.'

I opened the boot and grabbed Dave's bag. 'And after lunch, we'd better fit you out for a *gho*.'

'A what?'

'The national costume. I assume you'll want to wear it to the *tsetchu* festival tomorrow.'

Kinley came out to drive us down to the meeting point, but stopped when she saw Dave.

'Oh, no! You can't go like that.'

He was wearing a summer *gho* I'd bought in haste when the weather warmed up. It was too small for me, but Dave was shorter with a stockier build. I'd shown him how you could use elbows to hold everything in place while you tied the belt, but in the end I'd had to help him get it right. It looked good to me. I didn't understand why Kinley was shocked.

'They won't let you in with short socks.' She sighed. 'It's too hot to wear a *gho*, but if you really want to, I'll lend you a pair of Kinga's.'

Once we were sorted out, we all rushed down to the new highway where Kinley's friends were waiting. They'd been generous enough to offer us one of the fifty places in the VIP stand and we'd felt it would have been rude to refuse the honour.

It was already seven in the morning, so we rushed through introductions, jumped back in the car and raced off to the *dzong*. Dominique went back to pick up her *taikwondo* friends that she'd already agreed to spend the day with, while Dave and I followed our hosts to join the line of people stretching hundreds of metres from the entrance.

Each person that passed me on the way to the back of the queue commented on my *gho* using the same words. 'You look very smart.' I'd had it tailored especially for the occasion. Unfortunately, the tailor had adjusted for my height, but forgotten to take into account my lack of girth and the sides wrapped so far around that they crossed at the back. Dominique had told me not to worry, that the colour set off my eyes so well that no one would be looking at the hem.

The line carried us through metal detectors and bag searches until we arrived in the main courtyard. *Dzongs* were both monasteries and government buildings and as the home of both the central government and the central monastic body, this one was huge. The white walls of the central temple stood twenty metres tall and balconies on the surrounding buildings were tiered four high, all swarming with people. Red tiles rooved each building, just above designs in reds and yellows.

Thousands of revellers sat in the courtyard around an open square, a stage for the dancers, leaving a narrow path for people to walk clockwise around it. Bright colours filled the *dzong*. *Tsetchu* was an opportunity for everyone to put aside their work and gather. Historically, it was a time for young men and women to meet and court, so everyone wore their finest traditional clothes, some that had taken a whole year to dye, weave and embroider.

Our stand, covered in a monastery-yellow awning, sat ten metres from the square and looked across at a wide set of stairs, red with robed monks. A couple of men in technicolour *ghos*, traditional knee-high boots and demonic masks walked amongst the crowd, tapping people on the head with a large wooden phallus in exchange for a few coins. Our hosts explained that they were citizens collecting for the monastery and that *tsetchus* were a great source of money each year.

'They won't take their masks off in public until the last day of the festival, so everyone will be surprised to find out who they are. It means they can be unselfconscious for a few days.'

I looked back to see one of the demons holding the phallus as if it was his own and thrusting it into a lady's face. She reached up to grab it with only mild embarrassment.

Dancers from the Royal Academy of Performing Arts came on stage to open the festival, all in embroidered silk *kiras* of personalised bright colours. Rather than being folded and slung over one shoulder as usual, their *rachus*, the women's equivalent of the *kabne*, were wrapped around the torso to hang over both shoulders and cross at the back. They performed a couple of slow dances of the kind we'd done at Anna's farewell, but with an elegance I hadn't imagined was possible.

Sweat dripped down my neck as I watched for Dominique to arrive. I eventually saw her, with Sangay and others I didn't recognise, taking a seat on the other side of the courtyard among the local revellers. For all that Dave and I had an exceptional view, I wanted to be down with the crowd, sweltering in the sun, picnicking and enjoying their party. Our box seats separated us from the event as though we were watching it on television.

The women left the stage to be replaced by monks in multicoloured *ghos*, with wigs, crowns and white skirts. When the music started, they began spinning and jumping, all doing the same dance, but with no apparent coordination. The objective seemed to be to out-jump or out-spin the others.

The masked men returned again and again to the VIP stand and particularly to Dave and me. It made sense that they'd target the people able to afford seats in the stand, but it was in vain. I hadn't known this was part of the festival and hadn't brought any change. Dave still hadn't been to the bank and so was relying on handouts from me.

Each dance told the story of an event in the history of Bhutan, usually religious, but none of the people around us had the knowledge or desire to explain. The dances soon blended into one another. My interest came from wondering if someone would succumb to the heat and need to be carried off. None did.

Dominique, who'd been reading the news in our bedroom, came out to show us an article.

'It says that so many people went to the *tsetchu* that many locals were turned away.'

'What? All three days?'

'It doesn't go into specifics, but that's the way I read it. They'd been looking forward to it all year, making clothes specially, and then missed out on all three days. I feel bad.'

I did too. 'But it's not really our fault. They promote the *tsetchu* to tourists, but even they can't be the main problem. Thimphu's grown too much for the *dzong*.'

'Yeah. They say that too. Next year, it might be held in the stadium, but it just won't be the same.'

Dave's look made me feel like a whinger. 'That wasn't so bad,' he said.

I'd held off doing all the paperwork for our trip until Dave was here so that I could maliciously share the experience with him. We were planning to go east and needed road permits to cross each border between *dzongkhags*.

'Only because Dominique has done this so often that she knows the process. And we were lucky to find the woman in her office this morning.'

Dominique had arranged the signed request from her boss and told me to take copies of passports, visas and residency cards. She'd even filled out the road permit forms for the three of us. Dave and I had waited in line for a few minutes, but the woman at the Department of Immigration only took a few seconds to scan our papers, deem them correct and tell us to return in the afternoon.

'We've still got to get the Special Permits for entering the *dzongs* and temples. Hopefully that will be as easy.' Secretly, I hoped it wouldn't. I wanted Dave to experience the bureaucracy of the real Bhutan, but I also wanted him to have a taste of the work involved in getting him here.

The Ministry of Home and Cultural Affairs was up the hill and Dave was glad we had the car. Altitude was still a problem for him.

There were no signs inside the ministry, but I'd been there to prepare for our visit to Taktsang and headed directly for the door hidden behind the stairs on the second floor. A hall looped around to a room holding a desk covered in documents. A young man looked up between piles of papers stacked on the desk.

'What do you need?'

'We're going travelling and need Special Permits to visit restricted sites.'

'Show me your request.'

I handed the man our form, along with another letter from Dominique's boss and copies of relevant identification.

'Some of these are in other *dzongkhags*. Where is your road permit?'

'It's being done now.'

'Come back when you have it.'

I turned to Dave. 'And so it begins.'

Dave was struggling even before we reached Tango Goempa, a smaller temple at the end of the Thimphu valley famed as a meditation centre. Only three days into his visit, he claimed lack of oxygen, but he'd always had a problem on climbs.

'Wait here,' Sangay said, when we arrived at Tango. 'I'll go and find my brother.'

Families took great honour in having a member in a monastery and many families sent the second son off for training. When Sangay heard we were going to Tango, she had jumped at the chance to see her brother in his home.

She returned with a man just out of his teens who bowed his head to us. '*Kuzu zangpo la.*'

'*Kuzu zangpo la.* It's nice to meet you.'

'He doesn't speak much English,' said Sangay, 'but he said we can go and have a look at the temple if you like.'

The young monk led us to the best-kept building at the site. It looked like a traditional packed-mud house but for the wooden balcony and external walls covered in religious images. Some pictures were more freshly painted than others.

Dave hadn't seen a temple yet, so we took him through the process. Remove shoes before stepping over the tall wooden threshold to the worn floorboards inside. Once eyes adjust to the dim interior, prostrate three times each to the empty chair of the head monk and the altar. Stand before the altar and pray over a ten-ngultrum note, then place it on the altar. Cup hands and receive holy water from a monk. Sip it and wipe the rest over head.

The altar was covered in biscuits and lollies offered to the gods. One of two young monks already in the temple opened a packet of biscuits and passed some to his friend before taking a couple for himself. I tried not to smile at the idea that the action put Buddhist offerings on a par with whisky and cake left out for Santa Claus. Of course they couldn't let the food go to waste. I just hadn't thought that they'd be so obvious about it.

We planned to go further up the hill and Sangay's brother was given leave to escort us as far as the next monastery, a few hundred metres on, giving him more time to catch up with Sangay. The discussion was all in Dzongkha and I wondered what they talked about. The monk's Buddhist austerity gave as little clue as Sangay's smile.

The ascent became steeper shortly after he left us, but Sangay had found her energy. Now only Dave slowed us down. He'd rush ahead for fifty metres, then need to stop for fifteen minutes. When we saw a third monastery at three thousand six hundred metres, Dominique dashed ahead to prepare lunch. Dave and I arrived to find Dominique and Sangay picnicking in an outside courtyard, looking down the length of the valley. The view of lush greenery stretching all the way to Thimphu stopped conversation.

While we ate, an elderly monk appeared and put down a thermos and four cups, then disappeared without a word. It was a unique experience in our time in Bhutan, and clearly, to refuse would be to offend.

'Oh, it's soup,' said Dave, after taking a sip. 'I assumed it was tea.'

'Is that Murray Gunn?'

The accent on the other end of the line was American, but it wasn't a voice I recognised.

'Yes, it is. Who's this?'

'I got your number from Madeleine. Some friends of mine are making a movie and they're looking for a *chilip* to play the main role. I can't take the time off work, so I'm helping them find someone who can.'

My heartbeat sped up. Like many people, as a child I'd wanted to be an actor, but gave up when Mum pointed out that if I was too shy to go up on stage at a pantomime, then acting was probably not a good career choice. A Bhutanese film might be anonymous enough to be comfortable.

'My girlfriend's aunt is Dorji Wangmo,' he said.

'Who's that?'

'The most famous movie star in Bhutan and her uncle is a respected director. It will be a very high-profile role.'

I sat down, my legs weak. That eliminated my hope for anonymity, but it would be an amazing experience. Could I manage it? 'What's involved?'

'They want to start immediately and shoot for a month. It's a really aggressive schedule, I know, but it should be a lot of fun. They're great people.'

'I've got a friend visiting and we're heading to Bumthang tomorrow, so I can't meet them until next week. Even then, I'd need to wait until my friend leaves.'

'Oh. That might be too late. Do you know anyone else I might try?'

I didn't want to give the chance up, but it would be a relief not to have to be on display. 'You need a male expat who isn't employed. I only know of one other house husband.' I gave him Michael's contact details and said I'd call him when I got back to see how things had gone. If the role was meant to be mine, it would still be available. My own thought surprised me. It was close to admitting belief in *karma*.

'What was that about?' Dominique asked when I came in, probably with a goofy look on my face.

'Just someone wanting me to star in a Bhutanese movie with Dorji Wangmo.'

'Oh, I saw her in a movie while you were away. She's beautiful. And you'd get to kiss her. There's a lot of kissing in Bhutanese movies.'

I couldn't imagine that Bhutanese movies, generally modelled on Bollywood from what I'd heard, would have kissing, but why did she say this? Was she telling me to go and kiss other girls? Surely not. Hadn't she recently started to think of me as her husband? Then I saw that her eyes didn't match the smile. By voicing the fear, she was ensuring it would never come true.

Dave was in the driver's seat as we came around the magic corner. Hours of rally driving over endless precipices had taken its toll on Dominique and me. Dominique sat in the passenger seat, eyes fixed on the road and with the window right down, needing the fresh air. She'd refused to close it even for the cold air of the three-thousand-metre passes. I shut my eyes, trying to relax into the corners as Dave had during his turns as passenger. Once again, as soon as the car began to swing, my eyes flew open and latched onto the dotted white line down the middle of the road. It seemed to be purely cosmetic as the tar was only one lane wide and to drive to the side of the line was to put one wheel constantly in the dirt. Even as we rounded the corner, a truck came the other way, forcing Dave to apply the Bhutanese swerve. I had confidence in his driving, but remained hypnotised by the white line, willing it to remain under the car.

We rounded another corner and a double gasp from the front brought me fully alert. My fingers dug into the seat back, as if my grip alone could save us from a long fall into the valley, too far below to see through the evening mist. But it was the view that had taken their breath away. We'd reached a junction in the valleys where a new river cut in from the left. On the far slope, still well below us, was a small plateau with a hill along the near edge. Trongsa. The ancient seat of the current royal family.

Trongsa Dzong was a slumbering dragon stretched out on the hill, its belly following the contours of the ridge. By the time we pulled over, mist had covered the castle, but soon gaps opened up, each showing a glimpse of the white monster with its scaly red back. We lost ourselves in time.

Dave had eaten his first traditional breakfast at the hotel. Mouthfuls of fried rice with chilli relish punctuated the increasing views of the *dzong* as the mist rose. Now, standing on the plateau, tucked between the *dzong* and the mountain, he was seeing his first archery contest.

'What are they shooting at?' he asked, looking in the same direction as the archer.

'Follow the line of people,' I said. They left a passage only about six metres wide for the archers to fire along. 'There's a small target at the other end, where the opposition are jumping around. On that white board.'

'Oh, yeah. I can just make it out. That's got to be more than a hundred metres away.'

An arrow left the bow. I watched it arc up before descending towards the scattering opposition. Then I lost it in the distance. Six men ran back onto the range, hooting and laughing. One mimed an archer looking in one direction while aiming in another.

The next shooter studiously ignored the mockery as he took his place at the front of a grassed platform. He nocked an arrow, then raised his bow to the target.

'Doesn't anyone ever get hurt?' asked Dave. 'The crowd is standing so close.'

'Occasionally,' said Dominique, 'but the archers are very accurate. According to my colleagues, only a couple of people have ever been seriously hurt. It's incredible when you think that there are hundreds of contests every day. And the injuries have all been from Olympic bows, not this traditional bamboo style.'

His face screwed up in concentration, the archer nocked the arrow and lifted the bow in one smooth motion. He released it immediately to fly high above the heads of the crowd.

Dominique watched the arrow soar as she continued. 'Apparently it's two points for hitting anywhere on the white post and one point for hitting the ground within a metre of the base.'

The arrow disappeared from sight and a cheer went up from the other end of the field. One of the opposition reached towards the white post, but it was the lack of mockery that told the story. This time it was the six archers near us who gathered to hoot and laugh. They then did a dance like those we'd done at Anna's farewell. Lined up with arms around each other's shoulders, they walked forward and back, turning gently – a victory dance more appropriate to lawn bowls champions.

The monks left the *dzong* while the police at the entrance checked our special permits, cheers erupting from the archery range behind us. They walked in one column, out a higher gate and along the hillside.

'It's Sunday,' the policeman said, as if that explained everything. For five minutes, the procession continued at a sedate walking pace, each monk a step behind the one before and still more appearing. I couldn't get my head around the idea that all these monks could live together in confined quarters.

Inside the main gate, we bumped into an elderly monk who'd stayed behind. He was walking in the same direction as the others, but stopped when we arrived and came over to mumble at us in Dzongkha.

'We don't have a guide,' I said, assuming that was what he'd asked. 'We live here.'

He shook his head, then gestured for us to follow him. We walked up a set of stone stairs to the upper courtyard. White walls rose around us, with a maze of stairs like a villa on the Greek islands.

He bade us wait at a set of double doors. We looked through a crack in the wood to see shadows of an altar.

'So much colour,' said Dave, pulling his eye away from the crack. 'I guess it makes up for the lack of TV and computers.'

I thought I knew how he felt. We'd just seen a traditional archery match played with bits of shaped bamboo and now we were standing in an ancient castle. 'Hundreds of monks live here. I'm sure they keep themselves entertained in their own way when they're not working. Who really needs technology?'

'Come and look at this.' Dominique was leaning over the parapet on the downhill side of the mountain. On a narrow flat below the wall, a group of young monks were lining up to throw stones underhand towards a fist-sized rock five metres away. They cheered when one landed his stone a few centimetres from the target. 'Technology just gets in the way of healthy living.'

The old monk returned a while later holding up his hands in resignation. No key. Come with me.

We followed him back down to another set of double doors which opened onto a pair of prayer wheels. Dominique and I stepped over the threshold and began to walk around, pulling the wheels with us.

Dave copied us with a grin that matched the monk's. The old man was obviously pleased that we'd known his customs.

When we'd each done three revolutions of both wheels, he pointed us up a set of wooden stairs, directing us along to the far end of the castle, then bowed his head. This is as far as I go.

Dominique and I looked at each other in excitement. We'd never been allowed to go up into the workings of a *dzong* before.

The stairs were almost as steep as a ship's and we had to hold on to the railings to keep our balance. We could make out more stairs in the dimness and Dominique decided to climb another set, but came down saying it was too black to see anything.

The darkness increased the further we walked, but a window further down gave us a target while our eyes adjusted to the dark. With no shoes, I could feel the path that centuries of feet had worn into the floorboards and wondered if that was how the monks found their way around or if they lit lamps. A low hum, almost too quiet to hear, encroached on the peace and grew in volume with each step. When we reached the window, I looked out and back to where we'd come from. The old monk was standing in the window of the prayer wheel room running an electric shaver over his chin.

A strong afternoon wind spread out over the Bumthang valley, one of the few flat areas in Bhutan. It was wide enough that the main street of Jakar, the largest town of this *dzongkhag,* ran across the valley rather than along it. We were glad for the wind on the climb to Jakar Dzong, perched on a hill overlooking the town. A child running down the stairs stopped to offer us the heart of a sunflower with half the seeds already missing. Never having seen a sunflower up close, I inspected it, pulling out a couple of seeds while Dominique and Dave went on.

'Thank you,' I said, handing the flower back but keeping the seeds.

'Keep it.' He handed the flower back to me.

'Are you sure?'

'I can get more.'

I watched him skip down the path, wondering if the *dzong* had inspired such generosity.

Dominique and Dave were already at the top of the steps, talking to a monk in his mid-twenties.

'You've been to Tango, then?' he asked. 'I was studying there for the last five years.'

Dominique looked delighted at being able to show off her knowledge. 'Do you specialise in meditation, then?'

'Yes. I came to Bumthang to teach meditation. Some of the younger monks don't realise how important it is and it's my job to help them reach the point that they do understand.'

'I've often tried to meditate,' I told him. 'I've never been very successful. There are too many distractions in our world. I always end up with a song going through my head or an urge to watch TV instead.'

He smiled and sighed. 'It's good to practise English. If you have time to talk, would you like to come and sit down? I can offer you a cup of tea.' He must have seen Dominique's face freeze, because he laughed. 'I guess you don't like *suja*. Not many westerners do. But I have some herbal tea, too.'

We agreed and followed him to a door off the main courtyard.

'My room.'

'I didn't think you had your own rooms,' I said. 'Don't you all sleep together?'

'We sleep down there.' He pointed through a large gate to the inner compound. 'Under the kitchen. But when we have family, they can stay in our rooms. And because Sundays are free, we can spend time in them then. I share this one with two friends.'

He ushered us through a kitchenette and we stopped just inside the next door, fumbling for a light switch. When it came on, we all stood in shock. A television sat on a chair with a DVD player underneath. A ghetto blaster stood on a shelf and pirated DVDs were scattered on the bed, but the real surprise was a poster of Britney Spears where normally a picture of the king would be.

'Monks are just people like you and me,' said the head of the livestock division in Bumthang.

Dominique had invited her colleagues to join us for dinner at the hotel, though in the small country town way they were more familiar with the restaurant than we were and acted like hosts.

'You have to remember that many of them don't choose to become monks. Their families can't support them or they want the honour that comes from having a monk in the family, so they're put in when they're only six years old. Sometimes, even younger. It's not surprising that they love the same things that any young man would.'

He was well educated and had studied abroad so I felt comfortable bringing up topics that I wouldn't normally raise. 'How do you feel about the clash between religion and agriculture?'

'What do you mean?' He lifted the bottle of Special Courier and poured me another splash.

I accepted gratefully. The flavour only seemed to improve since I'd tasted it at Anna's farewell. 'Dominique explained to me that cows need to have calves to lactate. It's obvious when you think about it, but I'm not really a farmer.'

He nodded for me to continue.

'But since you won't kill the calves, the cattle population is growing faster than it would in western countries. Then you have trouble feeding them and end up with sickly cows that don't produce good milk. Have I got that right?'

'That's certainly a problem and there's no easy answer. Buddhism is more than just a religion for us. It's part of our culture and we can't change the way we do things without changing who we are. It's true that if we killed some of the calves, then the ones that were left would be healthier, but the Bhutanese people wouldn't stand for it. And the farmers wouldn't go through with the culling, anyway.'

'But aren't those rules open to interpretation? It's about respecting all living things, right?'

'Yes. Every living being deserves the right to live life according to its *karma*.'

'And saying that it's their *karma* to be killed isn't a good answer. I know that. We don't have the right to take fate into our own hands.'

He nodded again.

'But do you ever use disinfectant in your bathroom?' I asked.

'Yes. Why?'

'Well, aren't you killing bacteria? Even cough medicine is trying to kill germs or a virus or whatever.'

'I don't think Buddha or his followers knew about bacteria, so it doesn't count. But I get your point. I think we have to walk a middle path.' His finger drew a line on the table between our glasses. 'We can't survive without meat – the land doesn't provide enough to feed everyone on vegetables – so we have to open our minds to the idea of killing animals. We just have to make sure that we only kill what we need to survive.'

'Right. Those are the laws of nature. A lioness only kills when she really needs to eat and nothing goes to waste. She brings down the weakest gazelle, which makes the gazelle herd stronger. And weaker prides don't make the kill so they die off and the race becomes stronger. The same applies to eagles hunting. The hunter respects its prey in the purest way possible.'

'I'm not sure that the Bhutanese people will see it that way.'

We'd left Jakar early in the afternoon, hoping to reach Trongsa before dark, but as soon as we neared the pass into the Trongsa valley, mist had enveloped us. It was so dense that it became a mirror under high beams and low beams only penetrated a couple of metres into the mist. I'd slowed down to ten kilometres per hour, but even then the Bhutanese swerve would be no use unless any oncoming cars were travelling as slowly as us. Keeping the white line to our right wasn't really an option because it would disappear unless it was in a direct beam. For once, no one laughed at me for driving slowly.

'It wasn't a big deal,' Dave assured Kuenga.

The first day back in Thimphu, I'd dragged him along to help out with some network issues they'd been having at RIM. It would be a good chance for him to see the Bhutanese at work, I'd told him. He'd agreed.

Wangdi was hunched in humility, bowing his head in Dave's presence. 'Sir was fantastic. He fixed it all. I don't think there'll be any more trouble, now.'

'As long as you keep the network clean of viruses,' Dave added. 'I just closed off all the ports you didn't need, especially the ones viruses usually use to get in.'

'Thank you Mr. David. I hope you wrote it all down, Wangdi.' Kuenga was the most conscientious Bhutanese I'd met as far as making sure a lesson was learnt properly.

Wangdi paled. 'Can sir give me his email address in case I have more problems?'

I revelled in the water flowing over me. It had been great to see Dave, but three weeks of being together all day was exhausting. Now he was gone and Dominique was at work, I would have the place to myself for a few hours. I went to turn the water off and the hot tap spun in my hand, water still gushing. I jumped out of the scalding stream.

Minutes later, now dressed, I opened the dividing door and called up to Kinley. There was no response. There was a tank on the roof, but I had no idea how to get to it and didn't like walking into their house uninvited, even if they did the same to us. Remembering another tank outside, I ran up the hill to have a look. It had a floating ball in the top like a toilet tank. I grabbed a bent stick and placed it to trick the mechanism into thinking the tank was full, stopping the inflow from further up the mountain.

But that would only mean that the stored water would keep flowing until there was none left. I had to stop it further downstream somehow. I was an engineer. Not a mechanical or plumbing engineer, but surely I could do something. I ran around the house, checking connections, looking for a way up to the tank on the roof. No solution came to mind.

Kinley pulled up in her car while I was removing the stick so that we wouldn't run out of water.

'Kinley, our tap has broken and I can't stop the water.'

'I don't have time. I'm running late. You can take care of it.'

'I tried. I shut the water off at the upper tank, but...'

She looked at me and sighed. 'Come and I'll show you where the roof tank is.'

It was at the top of a ladder leading up from inside the house, partially exposed to the elements and surrounded with drying chillies.

'This one goes to the hot water.'

I memorised the tap she pointed at and wrenched it closed.

'Now. Let's have a look at the shower.' After a quick glance, she walked into our kitchen, grabbed a plastic bag, then headed outside where she chose a fat stick from debris beneath a tree. Back inside, she pulled the shower head off, twisted the plastic around the stick and shoved it into the pipe. 'You can turn the water back on now. That should hold. Now, I have to go. I'm late for a funeral.'

'I wonder how the preparations are going for the movie,' I said as I changed down to second gear and threw the car around a corner. 'They must have met Michael by now. They'll probably ask us both in for an audition.' The next corner was gentle, so I shifted up to third and kept accelerating until I'd passed fifty. Then back to second for the following corner, braking when I saw headlights coming the other way. The Bhutanese swerve was easy after taking a thousand corners on the trip east. Now I could see why everyone had laughed at me.

'I'd really like to take the role now, and I'm sure that I can act better than Michael. I don't think he's ever been on stage before. I have, even if they were bit parts. They'll make their own decision when they audition us, of course.' I pulled the Bhutanese swerve again before I realised that Dominique hadn't said anything. She was probably surprised at my confidence. She'd never seen me act.

'You're quiet tonight.' When there was no response, I took my eyes off the road long enough to see Dominique's knuckles white on the door handle.

Dominique was silent for the walk from the car to the Four Seasons restaurant. Part of me revelled in the reversal of roles, but not enough to laugh at her. Perhaps we'd both drive more carefully after tonight.

A yellow glow stunned all thoughts from my head as soon as we walked through the door. Michael and May looked up.

Michael was the first to speak. 'Murray, Dominique, welcome back. I've got to thank you for passing this opportunity on, Murray. It's going to be so much fun.'

It took a moment for me to realise what he meant. 'You've got the part already?'

'Yep. I met them a couple of days after you left and they offered it to me straight away.'

'What? No audition?'

'No. They just wanted to make sure we could get on well together. And apparently the character's name is Michael, so they took it as a sign.'

I pulled out a chair and dropped heavily onto it. So, fate had decided. *Karma* had something else in store for me.

Dominique asked the obvious question before I could find my voice again. 'But what about your hair?'

Michael ran his hand through the yellow glow. 'They said I didn't look enough like a foreigner. They really wanted someone with blond hair, so they asked me to dye it. This is how it came out.'

A shape moved in the corner of my eye and I looked up to see the owner of the restaurant at Centrepoint.

'Here you are, sir. One *oyakodon*.' She made a point of cooking for foreign guests herself because we were known to have higher expectations. Today I'd chosen a Japanese bowl of chicken and rice, laced with chilli for a Bhutanese twist. 'And where is madam?'

'She's out in the field somewhere visiting farmers. I can't keep track. She'll be back in a few days, though.'

After a few pleasantries, she headed back to the kitchen to check on the staff and I turned to the newspaper. The main story was that the prince had visited another village to discuss the new constitution with his people as both he and the king had been doing for months. The monarchy had been in place for a century and the current king had been working towards democracy since he was crowned at sixteen.

These royals were probably the first monarchs in the world to ever go on a publicity tour to gain support for a revolution. From the questions asked, it was clear that the people had read the constitution, but they didn't understand it. If the king said they needed a government voted by the people then they wouldn't question his wisdom, but could the constitution please be changed so that the king didn't have to retire at sixty five?

I sat in our cosy corner listening to one side of the conversation Dominique was having with Dorina to make last-minute plans. The following morning, we'd begin a ten-day walk from Paro to Punakha. It was the first part of the Snowman Trek. The warm-up.

'Three hundred ngultrum per day for a riding horse? But that's three times the price of the pack horses.'

I did a quick calculation in my head. It came to about US$100 for the one horse. We were trying to do this cheaply, avoiding the expenses that tourists had to pay for. Without special tents, tables and chairs or gourmet meals, we could make do with four horses rather than the ten or twelve a similar tour group would require. That also meant one horseman rather than two or three and we'd all act as camp helpers to avoid the need to hire someone for that role. And Dorina's friend Karma was giving us a good rate on his services as a guide. It still ended up costing more money than Dominique and I were comfortable paying.

'Hang on. Let me ask Murray.' She raised her voice. 'Murray, how do you feel about paying three thousand *Nu* for a riding horse?'

Thoughts crashed in my head. I had no intention of riding if I didn't have to. It was really a backup in case something happened to someone. Not me specifically. It didn't make sense to go on such a hard trek without some form of redundancy. Why should it be my choice? Anyone might need to ride it and the horse could share the weight of the packs if we needed to move faster. It made sense in every way.

'Don't you think we should have some level of extra support for a trek like this?'

'It's up to you, Murray. You're the one with the bad knee.'

No one else saw the need for caution. They saw it as a crutch for me. Perhaps it was. For the man who'd been hiking up to twenty times each year all through high school, who'd done some of the best treks in the world, who'd cycled most of the way from Brisbane to Sydney. A man in his mid-thirties, already reduced to needing a riding horse on a trek.

'I say yes.'

Those words were probably the hardest I've had to say in all my life. So much pride discarded in three little words. I'm getting old, they said. I'm not capable of adventuring any more. I'm too weak to keep up with my wife. Suddenly Dominique was holding me.

'It's okay, Murray. We're going to have a great trek.'

I realised I was sobbing, a whole year of bottled-up fear and frustration pouring out in a stream of tears. It was unstoppable.

'Your knee will be fine and you won't need the horse. You'll come back confident and happy and we'll start planning the next trip. We'll be happy together. You'll see.'

She held me until I was dry, making promises of a bright future.

Karma caught us up and bade us wait for the horsemen. He took a seat on a rock beside Dorina.

'It's okay,' he said. 'They were only an hour late. We'll still make good time.'

'They?' she asked. 'I thought we were only getting one.'

'He's brought his cousin as an apprentice. You pay for the horses, not for the horsemen, so it's no extra cost.'

'But what about food?'

'We have enough.'

Dorina frowned. 'I hope they're hurrying, Karma. We have a tight schedule. I can't afford to be even one day late and it all depends on these first three days.'

We had to make it over the first pass in three days, but that meant doing a three-day walk in two and skipping the rest day tourists took at Jangothang to acclimatise to the altitude before attempting that pass.

'Shhh...' Karma held his finger to his lips, mimicking the western gesture.

Dorina might have been the official leader, but it was clear to the rest of us who was in control.

'But, Karma, we have to keep walking. We can't–'

'Shhh...'

'No, I won't–'

'Shhh...'

Karma saw we were laughing at their antics and winked. Dorina subsided momentarily, turning back to sit straight, head bent in thought.

'Karma, there's not enough–'

'Shhh...'

'Why do the Indian army have a base here?' I asked. We'd just gone past a checkpoint, Karma passing all our papers through a rigorous inspection. 'Shouldn't the Bhutanese police be doing that?'

'See that ridge?' He pointed to the west, where the slope we were on met the skyline a couple of thousand metres away. 'That's Tibet. The border used to be down here, where we are, but before we became a monarchy, the Bhutanese got sick of all the invasions and pushed the Tibetans back up there.'

It struck me as ironic that Tibet cried foul play at China marching in and taking control of their country when Tibet had spent the previous three centuries trying to conquer Bhutan, sometimes under the command of a Dalai Lama. Bhutan, in its turn, had annexed Cooch Behar, a small southern kingdom, in the eighteenth century. Even the most peaceful countries can't claim clean hands.

'But the Indians?'

'With China so close, Bhutan needed some protection. We're too small to be able to defend ourselves against both India and China, so we chose a side. The Indian army set up a presence here to monitor Chinese activity. Our king wants them out now, but he can't really ask that without jeopardising our good relationship with India.'

When we moved off, I was in the lead, which meant no time for thinking further on the issue. I needed to keep Dorina's pace if we wanted to reach Jangothang the next day.

'There's a better campsite up further,' said Dorina. 'It's only an hour away. I remember it.'

Karma was in control again. 'Dorina, it's getting dark and we can't push the horses too hard on the first day. It might ruin them for the rest of the trip. And this is a good camp site.'

'But the next camp site is just as good and it's only an hour away. Ask the horsemen.'

'I will ask the horsemen, but it will be their choice. They know the horses. Here they are now.'

We all turned to see two young men appear with four small horses and a mule. Karma moved off to greet them.

'Well?' asked Dorina when he returned a few minutes later.

'We camp here tonight.'

Dorina slumped. 'There goes our plan then. Unless we get up really early tomorrow.'

A cheeky glint appeared in Karma's eye. 'They said they've never seen *chilips* walk so fast. They said at this rate, we would reach Jangothang by tomorrow evening and asked me to see if you were up to it.'

Dominique cannoned into my back when I emerged from the forest. I hadn't realised that I'd stopped.

'Move, Murray. We all want to see.'

Directly in front of us was a tourist group lazing around their camp, yaks grazing nearby. Above them towered a conical peak, white from base to summit and framed by the slopes of nearby hills which cut the shape to a white diamond. Jomolhari! It was 7,314 metres tall and the most sacred mountain in Bhutan, according to Karma.

Dorina stepped out from the trees, puffing. 'My god, you people walk fast. I had a hard time even keeping up with...'

Jomolhari was like that. There was nothing to say when you saw it. No need to talk. We were standing at 4,000 metres, making the peak nearly the distance above us as the height of Mount Fuji above its base. But where the Japanese peak was a tourist attraction climbed by thousands every day, Jomolhari had only been climbed once and was now off limits. Where in Japan, sacred was a reason for pilgrimages and souvenir shops, in Bhutan it meant a pristine environment to be admired from a distance.

Karma, with the ever-present cheeky glint in his eye, joined us just ahead of the horses. 'Haven't you ever seen a mountain before? Come on. Let's get camp set up.'

I awoke the next morning at 5:30 to Karma's chanting. He'd be in the kitchen tent getting breakfast, but there was no chance he'd let us help so I lay there listening to the peaceful sound. It was about five minutes before I remembered that we were at Jangothang and dawn was known as the best time.

'Dominique. It's after dawn. Wake up. We have to look at the sunrise on Jomolhari.'

Not a great sleeper even in our own bed, Dominique had it tough camping. I could barely make out her words through the hood she'd pulled over her face. 'I'll stay here. Tell me if it's worth getting up for.'

'Fine.' I rugged up, unzipped the tent and stepped out into the morning chill.

'So? Is it worth it? Murray? Murray?'

When she climbed out, wrapped in fleece and wool, she found me still standing, watching, mouth hanging open. It was the same scene we'd had the evening before, but with the sunrise colours wrapped around the mountain. Dominique sank back into my arms and we stood there until the colours had faded into the ice. Karma called us for breakfast and for the first time I noticed that the others had risen to see the view too.

The pass was just ahead of us. At 4,870 metres, it was the highest I'd ever been in my life and there were higher passes to come.

'How's your head, Murray?' asked Dominique when she caught up to me where I'd stopped just short of the summit.

'Fine. It's not even a real headache. More like the idea of one. As long as we get down quickly, it won't be a problem.'

I was just about to take a step when a decorative red plume appeared in the pass, pushed up by a black head. Yaks are known for erratic behaviour when spooked, so we all moved off the path. The yaks would choose their own routes, but it was better not to be on any worn tracks.

A stream of ten large black beasts continued past us, all walking slowly and panting. They looked like cows, but the shaggy hair on their torsos dragged along the ground, as did some of their tongues.

'It's too early in the year for them to be down so low,' said Karma, coming up from behind. Like the rest of us, he wore many layers of fleece and huddled against the cold. 'How's your knee, Murray? Do you want to wait for the horse to carry you down?'

I had little pride left after my cry before departure. 'I'll see. I think I'll walk as much as I can. If the horses pass us, I'll ride then.'

Dorina arrived back from the other camp and began rummaging through her pack. 'Bad news for them.'

The group we'd camped near the previous night had made the journey over the pass with us, but the single rest day hadn't been sufficient for one man.

'They thought he'd get better once he reached the lower altitudes again, but he spent the night throwing up and they can't rouse him this morning.'

When altitude sickness strikes, the only cure is to descend.

'So, are they going to take him back over the same pass? How else can they get out?'

She triumphantly pulled out a packet of Panadol. 'Apparently there's a lower pass leading directly back to Thimphu. They'll have to throw him over a yak and carry him out that way. But they all have to go. Even the ones that are still healthy.'

I looked back at the camp, hoping he'd be okay, but mostly feeling glad it wasn't me.

I leaned back as the horse stepped off a larger rock. Tsencho Wangdi, the younger horseman, watched me with interest. 'What do you do that for?'

'Lean back? It's better for balance. Mine and the horse's too, I think.'

'Do you know how to ride a horse?'

'Of course.' I'd first ridden when I was six and had regularly galloped along trails on our holiday farm when I was growing up.

'You're the first person I've met who knows how to ride a horse.'

'Surely you do, too. You have a riding horse, after all.'

'It's just for leading tourists on. I've never ridden it. Do you know the sounds to make?'

'Yep. This means go.' I clicked my tongue and nearly lost my balance as the horse stopped under me. When he'd stopped laughing Tsencho Wangdi said, 'No. That means stop in Bhutan. Go is "hup".'

I sat across from the baby-faced boy, staring into the flames. 'Tsencho, isn't it illegal to light fires out here?'

He relaxed back onto a log. 'It is, but no one will tell. Karma's already been to talk to the other guides and they're going to make their own.'

'What's the law against fires for? We're at the top of the tree line, so I can't imagine that bush fires are a real risk.'

'No. I think it's more that they're worried about losing the forest. But if we only take the dead wood, who cares?'

Dominique joined us, huddling in her fleece. 'How old are you, Tsencho?'

'Seventeen.'

'Your English is very good. Did you go to school?'

'Yes. I got to year seven.'

'So you've been a horseman for a while, then?'

'No. I only just finished school. I was in year seven for many years.'

'I guess you didn't like it much,' I added.

'It was okay. I was really good at English and Maths, but not much good at anything else. I wanted to keep going, but my mother's on her own and she needs someone to help her take care of the farm.'

'Do you have a horse farm like your cousin?'

'No. Only Tsen Tshering has horses in my family, but he's going to help me start my own business. I'll save up money from helping him and buy a couple of mares. Then I'll rent a donkey to mate with the mares so I can get some mules. They're stronger and they live longer than ordinary horses.'

'But they're sterile.'

'Yes, but I'll use them on tourist trips to save up money for more mares and maybe rent a stud horse. In seven years, when I'm as old as Tsen Tshering, I want to have as many horses as him. Unless something better comes along.'

I looked over at Tsen Tshering's weathered face. He was only twenty four?

'Something better? It sounds like a good life to me.'

Tsencho poked at the fire again. 'It's alright for you. Going on a ten-day hike is a holiday. You can sit back at the end of the day and look at the mountains, then go back to your jobs in an office.' He held up a flaming stick. 'This is our life. We have to come up here no matter what the weather's like and we do the same trails over and over until our feet are sore. And we can never go anywhere else. There's no holiday for us.'

We spent the next day walking along ridges well above the tree line. I wasn't fond of the stark landscape, but couldn't deny that it had its own beauty. One stretch of mountain we passed by was broken in vertical sheers, each tapering section angled so that some sheltered faces were white with snow. Others facing the sun showed the natural grey of the rock and still others were black with what I assumed was a kind of moss.

Beyond that, we turned a corner and descended into a valley occupied by a tiny village. It sat at the base of a cliff some five hundred metres tall and a backdrop of peaks over seven thousand metres high. It was surrounded by fields of about a hundred square metres, each boxed in by hip-high stone walls.

'This is the first sign I've seen of real care,' said Dominique as we approached the first wall. 'Most farmers in Bhutan let their cattle roam free and use the same fields for their crops year after year, but these people rotate their crops and use walls to separate the fields.'

'And presumably they stop cattle from damaging the crops.' Dominique had told me how the lack of rotation meant that worms which attacked the cattle expelled their eggs with the manure, only to have the larvae thrive in the rice fields so the cows swallowed the new generation. The cycle was self-perpetuating.

But Dominique wasn't listening. She was leaning over the wall to look at the grass below. 'Look. They've even sewn clover here to improve the retention of nitrogen, so they don't have to rotate the crops so often. Someone must have been here to show them, but they're the only people in Bhutan who've actually listened.'

'Maybe other villages up here will listen if you come to help them.'

Dominique moved off, grinning. 'Maybe they will.'

We passed a number of women working in the fields and I wondered where the men were until we reached the village. There, a couple of men sat with their legs circled protectively around pieces of canvas piled with meat. Each was using a machete to chop the meat into little pieces while dogs lay nearby, drooling. I asked Karma how the meat became available.

'Yaks sometimes fall off cliffs.'

I wasn't sure if this was another example of his cheeky sense of humour, but it didn't really matter. Whether the yak fell or was pushed, this seemed to be an example of my definition of respect. These people, I was sure, would only take what they needed.

I awoke the next morning with a sore throat. Stepping out of our tent, I found the ground covered in frost but for a single bare patch about the size of a rucksack. Could it have something to do with the yak we'd heard rutting nearby during the night? Dominique had clung to me in fear for an hour before we heard a dog we'd picked up in the last village chase it away.

The sound of Karma chanting led me to the kitchen tent. Before I ducked in, I noticed Tsencho reviving the fire. Beside him lay our new dog, a large portion of its black fur covered in frost. It was a perfect match for the blank patch by our tent.

'Morning, Karma. Can I give our guard dog a scrap?'

'Best not. It'll go home eventually.'

Karma stopped us. 'Okay. It's time for a vote. We would normally camp further up so we don't have to climb so far to the high peak tomorrow, but the weather's getting worse and it's going to be dark early today. There's another good campsite just up ahead.'

'We should go higher,' said Dorina. 'We can't afford to be late. I have to be back in five days to take care of the children.'

Madeleine had been nursing a cold over the last few days. 'I'd prefer to stay down here. I could do with one more night of good rest.'

Dominique looked at me. 'How are you coping?'

'I'm for staying here, but I'll manage if you want to go up today.' I'd ridden the horse today for the second time, but not because of my knee. I'd caught Madeleine's cold and I simply didn't have the energy reserves I needed to stay ahead of the horsemen.

'Let's stay here, then.'

Karma nodded while Dorina muttered about time, then began the short climb to our campsite.

I crawled into our tent as soon as it was up. Outside, Dominique took Tsencho through some *taikwondo* movements, much to the amusement of the rest of the group. I was already asleep when they called me for dinner.

They let me leave first. Fever or not, I was determined to make it to the high pass on my own. The *Lonely Planet* stated that the walk to the Sinche La pass is the hardest walk of the trek. Perhaps it was my delirium, but the day went very quickly. I barely noticed the group coming the other way or that our dog turned around to follow them back home. Once we'd done the first climb, we spent an hour in a protected valley, looking at the pass at the end. All too soon, we were there.

At 5,015 metres above sea level, it was as high as I ever wanted to go in my life. I looked around at the mountains, both shiny and murky, and revelled in the achievement of reaching this height. Snow blew in behind us, adding to the stark beauty. Still, I thought, give me forest and oxygen any day.

'You go on ahead,' Dominique said, rubbing her red nose against mine. 'I'm going to go a little higher. I love it up here.'

'Where are you going?'

She pointed to my left. 'At least up to where Dorina's meditating. From there, who knows?'

Snow continued to fall while we were having lunch. Karma had found a big rock to shelter behind, but the wind still found its way under all my layers of fleece.

'Another day,' said Karma, looking up at the pass, 'and I don't think we'd have been able to cross. We were very lucky, but we made it. It's mostly downhill from here, all below the tree line from tomorrow.'

A Laya woman who'd joined us grinned at the exchange. She didn't speak English, but seemed to like hearing our conversation. Layaps were famous for their beauty, though Tsencho didn't agree. He'd been telling us all trip that we'd be disappointed and now I saw why. Appearing forty in every other way, her face was as sun-scarred and wrinkled as a seventy-year-old.

'See what I mean? They're all like that. Thimphu women are much prettier.'

'Why does everyone say that they're so beautiful, then? Are they being sarcastic?'

Tsencho shrugged. 'Come on. We caught you early today, but it's better that you ride and we have to get the camp set up before the weather gets worse.'

I looked up from helping Tsen Tshering to see Karma and Dorina approaching.

'Dominique had a fall,' said Dorina. 'You'd better go and help her.'

I jumped up and ran back up the hill to where Madeleine was supporting Dominique. As soon as I arrived, Madeleine passed her over to me and moved off at her normal pace.

'Don't touch me.' The only thing Dominique hated more than the idea that I might be weak was showing her own weaknesses.

I stepped back. 'What happened?'

Her glare held fire. Eventually, she looked away and tried taking a step on her own. Pain flooded her face, tears spilled and her breathing came in gasps.

I stepped in to support her again and this time she grabbed my arm. 'Tell me,' I said.

She sighed before answering. 'I was so happy. I was at the top of the world with all those beautiful mountains around me. I was so happy that I ran down the mountain, just feeling the joy of being alive in such a beautiful place, but a rock turned under my bad ankle. I think I've broken it. Why can't I just be happy? Why does something have to go wrong whenever I'm happy? You deserve better than this, Murray. You should just leave.'

'Shhhh. I don't think you'd be walking at all if you'd broken it. It's probably a bad sprain. You just need to rest it for a few days.'

'But I can't rest it. We have to get back quickly for Dorina.'

'That's why we have the riding horse.'

This time, her glare held the sun. 'I'm not riding the horse.'

'I'm not riding the horse, Murray.'

Dorina, Madeleine and Karma had gone into the forest ahead of us. The horsemen would take another half an hour to tie all the luggage onto the beasts and catch us up. Dominique had one of my hiking sticks and held on to me with her other arm. She took small steps that weren't much better than not moving at all. Worse really, because each one sent a spasm of pain through her, some so badly that she pulled me off balance. At those times, the muscles in my knee screamed. Level ground had never caused me so much trouble.

I stopped and shook her arm off. 'Dominique, you can't do this. Look at you. This isn't fun any more. You're going to ruin your ankle entirely.'

She grabbed my arm again and started to walk. 'I didn't come on this trek to ride a horse.'

I gave in and helped her take a few more steps. 'Neither did I, but we can't always do what we want.' Then my own knee threatened to twist again and I stopped. 'I'm not going any further with you, Dominique. You have to stop.'

She pulled at me. 'Just a bit further. We can stop over there.'

'No. No further. We stop here.'

'Fine. I'll go on my own. Give me the other stick.'

I refused, but she turned and tried to walk regardless, getting only a couple of steps before shaking with pain.

'Enough.' It wasn't often that I shouted, but I couldn't help it now. 'Dominique, you can't do this. Learning when to give up was one of the hardest lessons of my life, but it's one I understand now and I'm giving it to you. If you walk the whole way, and I doubt you'd make it, you might never be able to use that foot again. Will it be worth missing out on years of *taikwondo* and trekking, just so you can say that you walked all the way, even on a bad ankle?'

While I yelled, Dominique turned and hobbled back to me. Tears streaming, she reached up to put her hands on my face. 'Murray, Murray, no. Just a little bit further, please.'

'Enough. I'm going back for the horses.'

She lowered herself to the ground, still crying. 'No, Murray. Don't go. I'll stay. I'll ride the horse when it comes. Just hold me.'

The nurse at Laya's Basic Health Unit backed me up. 'You should change the heat strips and re-strap the bandages every day. The less you walk on it, the better.'

'We have a riding horse she can use,' I told the nurse. 'At least until her ankle gets better.'

Dominique glared at me but stayed silent.

Karma had directed us to the BHU as soon as we reached Laya. The pretty young nurse contrasted greatly with the weathered faces we'd seen on the way into town. They'd been sitting outside their huts as we arrived, presenting ornaments decorated in turquoise and amber, the precious stones of Bhutan, for prices a fraction of what they sold for in Thimphu. As much as we'd love to have them, we couldn't stoop to buying family heirlooms. Karma agreed sadly. 'They don't know the value of what they give away.'

'Are you from Laya?' I asked the nurse as we were leaving.

'No. I'm from Thimphu, but since I've only just started work, I was assigned to Laya for a year and have to stay here even through the winter. Next year, I'll get a better assignment.'

'Is winter hard?'

'Very. Most of the villagers go down to Punakha for the season, but some are too old or sick to travel, so they stay here. I have to stay to look after them, make sure they have enough food, that sort of thing.' She laughed, an attempt to conquer fear. 'The doctor said that last year he had to climb out of his window because the snow had blocked his door, and then he had to dig to get into the houses where his patients were.'

Outside, the rest of the group were watching kids play soccer. The field, just in front of the school room, was lumpy if mostly level, and sat at the edge of the plateau. As we joined them, the ball was kicked free and headed towards the precipice. Ten boys raced to catch it before it went over.

'What happens if they're not quick enough?' I asked.

Karma looked at me. 'They have to walk two hours to reach the river and then they have to find it.'

'This will do.' Light rain had begun to fall and Karma wanted to get settled before it became harder.

We joined him and the horsemen in pulling the hessian bags off the horses, then helped Karma put up the kitchen tent while the horsemen saw to their charges. By now it was all a routine and we were glad to have the work to pass the time in the late afternoons. Besides, it took the edge off the cold that crept in as soon as we stopped walking.

I was pegging down the cover that served as both kitchen and home to the three Bhutanese when a group of pack horses trudged past.

'Was that a TV?' asked Madeleine.

'I thought so, too,' I said. 'What are they doing with all that stuff?'

Karma, Tsencho and Tsen Tshering were all grinning.

'They're smuggling goods from Tibet,' Karma said. 'It's always cheaper. Tonight we go shopping.'

It rained all the following day, a cold, soaking rain that sapped all the joy from the trip. We walked past a leech-infested hut that trekkers usually camped in, choosing instead to brave the bears in the forest. Our tents were still wet and leaking when we pitched them on the muddy track. Dominique and I were snuggled in our sleeping bags, trying to ignore the damp, when Tsencho called from outside our tent.

'Can I borrow a torch?'

I grabbed mine and passed it through the door. 'What's the matter?'

'The horses have run off. They're scared of the leeches.'

Dominique passed her lamp out. 'Better take them both. Unless we can help.'

'No. They know us and we can catch them if they haven't gone too far, but you might scare them even more.'

Through the gap in the door, I saw that Tsencho didn't even look wet.

'Has the rain stopped?'

'Yes, but it's started snowing now, which will just make them harder to find.'

Karma was in a good mood when we woke up the next morning, despite the snow still falling. I found him chanting happily over porridge.

'They found the horses, I see,' I said.

'Yep. They hadn't gone very far. It only took them a couple of hours. Did you hear the bear?'

'What? Last night? Was there really a bear here?'

Karma began laughing so hard I could barely follow his story. 'Madeleine came running in here just after they came back with the horses. She was still in her pyjamas, running barefoot through the snow, yelling, "Bear. Bear. Bear. There's a bear in my tent." I was scared, but I grabbed the machete and went outside with her.'

'What was it?'

'Some snow had piled on her tent and she woke up when it all slid off.'

Madeleine poked her head in the door. 'Are you making fun of me?'

Karma fell back onto his bed. 'Bear! Bear! Bear!'

Gasa Dzong appeared when we came around the ridge. Dominique and I looked at each other in relief. It had been the hardest day of the trip for both of us. The horsemen wouldn't risk the horses with the weight of a person on such a steep descent. We'd started in snow that morning and would soon finish in the tropical rainforest of Gasa.

Tsencho came running out of a shop as we walked through the town. He sat down just as we reached him and began to change his shoes for a brand new pair.

'They're exactly the same shoes,' Dominique observed.

'I always get the same ones. They're not good quality, but they're cheap. Only two hundred *Nu*.' About US$6.

I looked closely and decided that was probably all the stitched canvas and rubber was worth. 'How long do they last?'

'Only a couple of trips. They almost didn't make it this time.' He held up one of the old shoes to show the sole flapping loose.

'Why don't you get proper boots? They'd last much longer.'

'I can't afford them and they'd still wear out before I got my money's worth. These are best.'

I didn't like giving charity, but Tsencho had become a friend. Once we were out of earshot, I asked Dominique, 'Should we buy him a pair when we get back?'

'What would be the use? We'd just contribute to messing up the economy. Teach a man to fish, remember.'

Madeleine, still halfway through putting her tent up, got her camera out and took a photo of the row of Indian men. We'd hoped to stay in the huts, but they were full, so we delayed the bath in the hot springs to get the tents up and dry. The Indians, who were probably the reason all the huts were full, sat down to watch as though our work was the most fascinating thing they'd ever seen.

Karma had tried telling them in Hindi that we didn't appreciate the audience, but it had no effect. Nor did Madeleine's photo. I decided to try connecting with them.

Leaving Dominique to finish putting up our tent, I walked over and sat at the end of the row and began imitating them, turning it into an impression of a ping-pong clown from the fairs of my childhood; amazed expression, mouth open, head turning slowly to take in all the action. It got a laugh.

'What's your name?' I asked the young man next to me.

'Sandeep.'

'I'm Murray. Where are you from, Sandeep?'

'I come from Bengal.'

Dragging information out of him felt like an inquisition, but hopefully that would be enough to make them leave. 'What are you doing in Bhutan?'

'We're building the road to Gasa.'

'Is this your day off?'

'Yes.'

'Why are you staring at us?'

He shrugged.

'Well, maybe it's time you found something more interesting to do.'

None of the locals had been shy about undressing and showering, but the locals weren't being watched by the Indian men at every moment. The water gushed out of a spout in the top of a cubicle carved in the stone. I stood in the opening while Dominique stripped, rinsed off the days of accumulated sweat, washed her clothes and put them on again. She then stood in the entrance glaring at the Indians while I took my turn. They finally moved away.

When we were both ready, we hopped into the baths fully clothed and were soon joined by Madeleine and Dorina.

'Each one of these springs is meant to provide a different kind of healing,' Dorina explained. 'That one over there is for cancer, apparently. And the one just out of sight is for skin problems.'

'What's this one for?' I asked.

She looked up at the characters marked on the sign. 'I'm not sure. Eternal youth?'

A couple of the Indians walked past, staring openly at the clinging shirts of the women. The path ended at our bath. There was no reason for them to walk past.

'Bugger this.' Dorina stood up. 'I'm not sitting around to pose for these perverts.'

It was a huge relief to leave Gasa the next morning. The Indians had watched us pack, turning away as if they hadn't even noticed us when Karma began shouting at them. I eventually lost my temper and approached them again.

'Look. You're welcome to help, or even just make conversation, but staring is rude. Bugger off.'

The result was the same. They simply turned their backs and talked among themselves until I returned to my packing. We'd left the horses hobbled outside the compound for the night and would have appreciated help carrying all our gear back to load them up, but that was never offered.

By the time I'd done my fourth trip, the last, Tsencho and Tsen Tshering had rounded up the horses and were checking their wounds. Blood matted their fur and I saw Tsencho pick one leech off that had swollen to the size of a large chilli.

We moved quickly along the trail, our spirits improving as the sun rose higher and we neared the road where our driver awaited. At one point, we passed a large American woman leaning on a staff, puffing loudly.

'I'm going to die in Bhutan,' she said between breaths.

'How far are you going?'

'Laya.'

None of us had the heart to tell her that she was only two hours into a four-day walk that was going to get a lot steeper and then she'd have to come back down. The laugh it gave us carried us all the way to the waiting truck.

Before we knew what was happening we were piled in and heading home. Out the back window, we could see Tsen Tshering and Tsencho turning the horses around for the trek back to Paro, this time without a tent.

I bumped into Pemba as I was hanging out our clothes the next morning and told him all about the trek. But he'd had the government reorientation while we were away and I was more interested in hearing about that.

'They do it to help Bhutanese students who come back from studying abroad,' he told me. 'We had to relearn all the protocols like who to show respect to and how much, and what all the different coloured *kabnes* mean. It's amazing how much you can forget while you're away.'

'Do they talk about jobs?'

'Yes. They said that there are too many graduates now for the government to employ everyone. They used to, you know. But there were over five hundred students who'd graduated this year and they only have jobs for two hundred.'

'So what are they suggesting?'

'They told us that Bhutan really needs to build the private sector and that's the best way we can help the country. Most of my friends are upset, but not me. I really respect my dad and I want to learn as much from him as I can. He's putting me in charge of the shoe shop in town and I'm going back to India next week to try to find some more fashionable stuff. Right now, we just get sent all the items that our suppliers can't sell in India.'

I congratulated him on his new job and was just about to go back inside when I remembered Paprika. 'By the way, do you know why the cat's changed colour? He's all grey now.'

'Oh, yes. Sorry about that. It was cold while you were away, but he wouldn't come up to our place because he's scared of our cat. Anyway, my grandmother is staying here again and she won't bathe in water heated by electricity. She thinks it's contaminated. So we put a tub in the shed and boiled all the water in the fireplace there. I guess it stayed warm. Your cat's been sleeping in the ashes.'

Dochu La had shrugged off its ever-present mist to show us a line of snow caps stretching away to the east. While the others stopped to enjoy the view, I was introduced to our host for the day.

Dorji Wangmo looked up at me with beautiful charcoal eyes and I immediately fell for the movie star. She had the toned curves that I liked, her round face was unblemished, her smile natural and her hair a glossy black.

'Bloody hell,' she said. 'I'm glad it was Michael and not you.' Before I'd even had a chance to react to the uncivil greeting, she'd lifted my arms over her head, slung me over her back and begun to walk, dragging my feet in the dirt. She only made it a few steps before straightening up and letting me stand again. 'I have to do that with Michael. It's a key part of the plot, but you're too tall.'

'I think I'm glad, too,' I said, catching my breath.

'I see you've met my co-star.'

I spun around to see Michael. 'We were just getting acquainted. She seems to like you.'

'It's mutual. She's amazing. She wrote the story – it's not really a script – she wrote the music, she can really act and sing and she helps Kinley with the direction.'

'I'll leave you two to catch up,' said Dorji Wangmo. 'We need to find an appropriate location to shoot.'

I grinned at Michael's yellow hair, now black at the roots. 'So you've been having fun, I guess.'

'Oh, it's been a great experience, but I'm getting sick of eating *ema datshi* three times a day.'

'Where have you been?'

'We've been camping in a yak hut up near Pele La on the way to Trongsa. I'm playing a tourist who gets lost. Dorji Wangmo and her niece are yak herders who rescue me.' He looked around at the gathered expats. 'Where's Dominique? Couldn't she make it?'

'No. She doesn't stop working these days. She's helping the marketing group on top of everything else. They're trying to build a market for the locally produced cheese.'

'Good for her, but it's a shame she's not here. Well, at least we've got plenty of *chilips* for the scene.'

'Sir Michael,' Kinley Dorji, the director, called out from the edge of the forest.

'Sir Michael? They call you Sir Michael?'

Michael grimaced. 'It used to be just 'sir,' but when I told them to call me Michael, all they did was add my name. I've given up trying to correct them now.'

'Sir Michael. We've found a good place. Please get everyone together and follow us.'

When we came to a clearing, we were directed to sit in a circle to hear the actor playing the guide give instructions.

Michael rushed up behind us and handed Kinley a note. 'I think he'd say something like this.'

'Great.' Kinley passed the note to the actor. 'Dorji. Memorise this.'

'Okay. I'm ready,' he said, after a few minutes during which Kinley had set up the cameras.

'Great. Action!'

'Listen up, everyone. It's very important that we all stick together. You don't know the area and it's easy to get lost up here and very difficult to search. If you... I forgot my lines.'

We eventually wrote key points on a card and held it up for him, but the speech was to be one of the longest in the film and it was ten takes and half an hour before Kinley was satisfied.

'Okay. That will do. Now, we'll skip to the point after Michael gets lost. Everyone stand up. The assistant guides will come up that hill and Dorji, you'll do a count and realise someone's missing.'

We all stood around watching the ad-libbed exchange and the rising panic until two of the guides ran back to search. Again, Kinley asked for a second take, just in case. Then it was our turn again.

'Michael was walking behind you all, but in front of the last guides. He stopped to look at some flowers and kept walking up the main trail, but you'd all gone down a side track. Now that the guides have all arrived, you realise that Michael's missing. Action!'

'Where's Michael? Oh, where could he be?' Hands were wrung melodramatically.

'What if something's happened to him?'

'Oh, poor Michael.'

By the time the camera panned around to me, I was so horrified by the contrived acting and worried that I'd look just as silly that I chose not to speak. An anguished expression would have to do.

Apparently it did.

'Cut. Beautiful. Now I just need the two people with the loudest voices to start calling out to Michael. A man and a woman.' Two volunteers raised their hands. 'Okay, you'll both do. Action!'

A white scarf hung over the door to Yeshey's new office.

'That looks like a temple scarf,' I said as I entered, 'like the one on our car's rear view mirror.' We'd had to wind ours around the mirror support so I could see traffic on the left when I drove.

Yeshey welcomed me in. 'It is. I got the company blessed on the weekend. I would have invited you to watch, but I knew you were busy filming.'

'Was the blessing a full *puja* with music and incense and everything?'

He nodded.

'I didn't know you were so religious.' Yeshey had always seemed much more worldly than other Bhutanese. 'And doesn't that conflict with the idea of making money?'

Yeshey sat down behind his large wood-veneer desk and I pulled up a chair opposite him.

'Even monks need money to live and for the butter in the prayer lamps. And if by their blessing they help me make money, then I'm likely to donate more to them. But you're right, I see Buddhism as part of our culture rather than believing in gods and black days, myself.'

'Did you have the *puja* on an auspicious day, then?'

'Of course. If my clients think that my company hasn't been blessed, or was started on an inauspicious day, they won't use my services even if they like me. If you want to work in Bhutan, you have to act Bhutanese.'

'When in Rome...'

'Exactly. Especially if you're Roman. So, do you like my new office?'

It was on the top floor of a modern complex, with views stretching down the valley towards our house and the temple on the hill.

'I do, but couldn't you have found something smaller? This place is big enough for ten people.'

'I've already got two staff and I plan to grow.'

I didn't doubt it. Working at DIT had given him a lot of inside knowledge and he seemed to have a good relationship with everyone in town.

'Until then, I've just got to cover the rent.' He named a price that equated to less than US$200 per month.

'Have you got anything lined up yet?'

'There are a couple of government contracts I'm going for, but it's going to be tough. Just to apply, I need to buy the tender document for about the same as my monthly rent, then I have to learn how to write a proposal.'

'What projects?'

'The main one is to put a wide area network into every *dzongkhag* office. Right now they all use dial-up, which is barely enough for email.'

'It sounds like it was a good time for you to get out of DIT.'

'The projects were only part of it. The main reason was that the next two years have been declared black years. If I didn't start my company now, it would be a long wait.'

'I know,' said Dominique, when I mentioned the two black years. 'They've brought the ground-breaking ceremony for our new office up to next month so that the building will have begun at an auspicious time.'

'So everyone will be trying to start relationships or companies or whatever in the next couple of months, then nothing.'

'Two years of relative quiet. Yep. I think it will be good for the economy.'

'Not just the economy. It could give the people time to catch up with the progress. The government could put attention into reducing crime and teaching people about the damage they're causing the environment by throwing rubbish into the rivers. But I don't get how they didn't know this before. They've had ample time to toss the dragon bones. Why did they suddenly discover the black years now?'

I could see suspicion forming on Dominique's face to match my own as I added, 'They say the king and the Je Kempo are good friends.'

'And the monks do the astrology. It would probably help them bring people's focus from money back to Buddhism.'

'It's engineered?'

'That or very fortuitous timing.'

'Is the king down there?' I asked.

Dominique squinted. 'I can't see him.'

'But he'd have to come to his own birthday celebrations, wouldn't he?'

The newspaper today had been twice as thick as usual with full-page ads from companies wishing the king a happy birthday. It was difficult to be sure if each was meant more as advertising or genuine homage.

'That might be him on the stage in yellow. Do you think we can get closer?'

I looked down at the thousands crowding the Changlimithang soccer field. Many were in traditional dress despite it being Saturday. 'Not easily. And it's their celebration. I don't need to see the king so badly.'

'I do. He's sooo handsome. Look. There's Michael.'

I followed her finger to see a yellow-haired man emerging from the crowd below us. By the time we reached him, the camera crew had appeared too.

'Sir Michael,' I said. 'This is the first time I've seen you in a *gho*.'

Michael scowled. 'Don't you start with the titles. It's for the movie. This is the last day of shooting.'

'You've been working on it for two months now. How do you feel?'

'Relieved. It's been great, but so long.'

Dorji Wangmo arrived and was introduced to Dominique.

'Is the king here today?' Dominique asked her.

'I don't think so. There'd be more security if he was, but he doesn't normally like these ceremonies. He's probably at his home, working.'

Kuenga stood in front of my desk. 'Murray, do you have time to work on a project?'

I looked up at him. 'It depends on how big it is. The students don't bother turning up to class much, so I don't think I'm any value there. A project might be better use of my time.'

Kuenga sighed. 'I'll have Tshering do something with the class. This is the first time we've run your subject, so they probably don't see it as very important, but the project is. The director wants a better inventory system to replace the paper process we have now. If we had an online system, he could get reports whenever he wanted.'

'Dominique doesn't know whether our visas will be renewed, but I can certainly make a start on it.'

'Great. I'll tell Thinley, the asset manager, to talk to you about what he needs. On another matter, I've just secured a grant by Ausaid for network training. It's enough money to send one of our staff to Australia.'

Here it comes, I thought. Dominique and other expats had often told me how their bosses took all the training opportunities, especially if they involved international travel. Training was knowledge and knowledge was power. More importantly, time away on business came with a daily service allowance, most of which found its way into the traveller's pocket. Dominique's boss would never send someone on training if he could take it himself. Now Kuenga was about to ask me how he could do this most cheaply so he could retain as much of the allowance as possible.

'Or I can pay for someone in Australia to come out here and give training. That way, we could organise for key staff from each ministry to join and train ten or twenty people for the price of one. I was thinking of your friend, Dave. Can you ask him if he'd be interested?'

I looked up from the database I was designing for the inventory system to see Sangay Wangchuk standing in front of me, chewing *doma* as usual.

'Hello, Mr. Murray. I had to come to RIM for a meeting, so I thought I'd come and see how you were doing.'

'It's good to see you, Sangay.' I looked at my watch. Almost noon. 'Do you have time for lunch?'

'A quick one. I'm sooo busy.'

As we walked to the cafeteria, I told him about the students' lack of interest in my technologies and the new project. He suggested that I keep the design open.

'All government departments have the same forms and the same rules, so if you develop a good system, you might be able to sell it to the other departments too.'

I put our lunches on my tab to be picked up by the director. Besides unrestricted use of the very slow internet and the unwanted honour of being called 'sir,' it was the only payment I received.

'But enough about me,' I said. 'What's happening at DIT now?'

'Ah, it's not good. Have you heard about Microsoft?'

'I know they were funding some communication centres in remote areas.'

'No, not that. We've been working with them on a project to create a Dzongkha font in Windows. It cost us half a million dollars.'

'That sounds great. What's the problem?'

'Microsoft changed the name. The Chinese government claimed that Dzongkha has affiliations with the Dalai Lama, so if Microsoft want to keep selling Windows in China, they can't use the name Dzongkha.'

'But that's ridiculous. There's no connection there at all, is there?'

'No, but Microsoft caved in to the demands. They've changed the name from Dzongkha to "Tibetan – Bhutan."'

'Why? That's making an even stronger connection between the two countries. It makes it seem like Bhutan is a state of Tibet.'

'Right. And it gets worse. They've changed every reference to Dzongkha in their products. Even Encarta must now call it "Tibetan – Bhutan."'

Pieces started falling into place. This could be the beginning of a passive political takeover. If China ever managed to annex Bhutan as they had Tibet, how loudly would the world cry out when their references implied that it had always been part of Tibet, which was now part of China? India might be the only country to put up a fight.

'Exactly,' said Sangay, as if he'd read my mind.

'Papers please,' demanded the customs officer.

I handed our passports, IDs and travel documents through the bars. '*Kuzu zangpo, la.*'

He looked up in surprise and smiled. '*Kuzu zangpo.* You live in Bhutan?'

'Yes,' Dominique said. 'In Thimphu. I work for the Department of Livestock.'

The officer pulled a handkerchief out of his *gho* and wiped his forehead. I watched as the beads of sweat formed again despite the electric fan blowing on his back. At the foothills of the Himalaya, even winter is hot and humid.

'Are you leaving or returning?'

'Leaving. I'm going to investigate the market for Bhutanese cheese in Kolkata.' She didn't mention that we'd tacked this trip onto our visit to Australia for Christmas so that we could avoid Druk Air charges in one direction at least.

The man filled in a couple of lines in his ledger, stamped our passports and passed them back to us. He wiped his forehead again as he said, 'You'll need to go to the Indian Immigration Centre through the gate and to the left.'

'How can he stand wearing a *gho* in this heat?' I asked Dominique as we walked towards the arch over the road and the cacophony beyond.

'He has to by law. It's cruel, isn't it? Imagine how hot it is in summer.'

The arched gate separating the twin towns of Phuentsholing and Jaigon was also the border between Bhutan and India. Bhutanese police were checking everyone coming the other way, but no one stopped us entering India. That attitude mirrored the environments. Phuentsholing on the Bhutanese side was clean, quiet and orderly. Jaigon was chaos. I pulled Dominique out of the path of a car. Its horn, joining all the others, was muffled in the heat. We moved around stalls that spilled onto the road, stepped over rotting debris, and tried to stay clear of the traffic.

I held my hand to my face to block the exhaust fumes and the smell of cow manure.

Dominique in turn pulled me away from a bull that, by virtue of size, weight and religion, claimed right of way. It was going in the same direction as us, creating a wake that sped our trip to the Immigration Centre.

I felt a touch on my arm and turned from the bus window to see a teenage girl leaning across the aisle towards me.

'Have you been touring Bhutan?' she asked.

'No. We live there,' I told her. 'You sound Bhutanese. How come you didn't get on the bus in Phuentsholing?'

After getting our passports stamped in both countries, we'd gone back to the post office on the Bhutanese side of the border to catch the bus.

'I'm Southern Bhutanese, but I'm not allowed to enter Bhutan.'

'Why not?'

The bus stopped to let on more passengers. Our driver was trying to fill every seat for the trip to Kolkata. All our luggage was on the roof, but new passengers dragged their bags into the aisles. Some even sat on their luggage for lack of another seat.

'The Bhutanese government kicked my family out in 1990 with lots of other Southern Bhutanese. They say that we're not really Bhutanese because we didn't have land deeds to say we'd been there for fifty years.'

'But you don't look old enough to remember Bhutan.'

'I don't. I wasn't even one year old when my parents had to flee.'

'So do you live in Jaigon, now?'

'No. School just finished so I came to visit my brother – he managed to get a job in Phuentsholing – and now I'm going back to the refugee camp to see my parents.'

'Where's the refugee camp?'

'In Nepal.'

'But if you're Southern Bhutanese, isn't your ancestry Nepali? Can't you live there normally?'

'No. They insist we're Bhutanese now, not Nepali.'

'That must be awful. How many people are in the camp?'

'About one hundred thousand, I heard, but some of them are proper Nepalis who thought we had better conditions than on the farms so they jumped the fences.'

I sat back to let the numbers sink in and Dominique leaned across me.

'Will you try to get a job in Bhutan when you finish school, like your brother? Do you want to go back?'

'I'd like to live in my home country again, but not while the king is in power. I won't go back until there's a democracy.'

I was lounging by the pool at my parents' house in Port Macquarie when Dad approached to spout news at me. 'The Bhutanese king has abdicated.'

'I think you heard it wrong, Dad. The crown prince will take over in 2008. It was probably just that.'

'No. I'm sure they said he'd handed over power already.'

I sighed and braved the heat to stand up. 'Let's check the internet.'

The internet seemed so fast in Australia after the dial-up speeds I'd become used to in Bhutan.

'Here it is.' I scanned the article. 'We're both right. He has begun handing over power, but he won't hand over the reins officially until 2008.'

Dominique and I both scrambled in out of the cold as soon as she opened our front door. The Bhutanese winter was a shock after the heat of an Australian Christmas and a night in Bangkok.

Dominique turned and snuggled up to me. 'It's good to be home again.' She stood on her toes for a kiss. 'I'm going to have a hot shower and get some dinner. Can we watch an episode of *Dark Angel* tonight?'

A clack behind us announced the arrival of Paprika through his flap.

'Only one episode? Promise?'

Paprika sat down beside us and started screaming, but he couldn't ruin our mood.

'To start with.'

I snorted. 'That means three again. We'll finish this series in a couple of weeks too.'

Another kiss. 'Then we'll just have to find something else to do.'

I watched her wiggle off to the bathroom then picked up a broom, thinking about the change that had come over her since she'd spent time with my friends and family. It was like I'd finally passed all the tests and was a valid husband. I hummed 'Great Southern Land' while I swept stones out of the hall and study. Whatever they were, they'd even found their way onto the desk.

Once the place was tidy again, I pulled down the DVD pouch from the shelves above our cosy corner and flicked through for *Dark Angel*. There was a gap, a missing disc in the Disney section. And another. And another. Someone had been in our house while we were in Australia, thrown stones around and taken our discs. What else had they taken? I rushed to the spare room to check that our laptops were still hidden away.

'Oh, Mr. Murray. I'm glad you're here. Perhaps you can see why my computer isn't working.'

Fixing computers at RIM was hardly my job, but I had always tried to help where I could. Besides, Thinley wasn't going to be much help in defining the requirements for an inventory system if he was distracted by other issues.

'Sure, Thinley. What's wrong?'

'It keeps giving this error message.'

'A full disk, huh? Well, let's see if you have anything you don't need.'

I ran the usual clean-ups, then began checking for large folders.

'Surely an Asset Manager doesn't need this.'

He looked over at the folder of porn I'd opened. 'No, no. I don't know what that's doing there. Ah, so many people use my computer, it's no wonder it breaks so much.'

I deleted the folder and showed him that he now had seventy five percent of his disk space back. His relief was so real that I wondered if the porn hadn't been his after all.

'Have you heard the news, Mr. Murray?' he said as I moved back to the seat on the opposite side of the desk. 'China is building roads into Bhutan again. Ah, always they stop when the king asks them to wait until the disputed borders are agreed to, but always they start again when we're not looking.'

'I didn't know they disputed the border.'

'Yes, yes, Mr. Murray. What we took when we pushed Tibet back, China now claims as theirs.'

Chinese takeover phase two.

'You Australians don't do manual labour, do you?'

The change of topic threw me. 'What? Of course we do. Who else is going to build our roads or fix our plumbing?'

'Oh, you're like China and India? They do manual labour. I thought Australia was advanced like Bhutan. We bring in Indians to do manual labour for us.'

Kinley was already hanging clothes on the line when I took ours out.

'Happy New Year, Kinley,' I said. 'I don't know if you actually celebrate new year.'

She tucked her *doma* into her cheek before replying. 'We do. Our new year is called Losa and it's at the beginning of February.'

'So what were all the stones in our house when we came back from holiday?'

She waved her hand in dismissal. 'Oh, that was just a *puja* to purify our house. The monks scatter the stones for cleansing.'

I moved to the other end of the long rope that hung over the dog's house and began to peg up our clothes. 'Kinley, do you know who came into our house while we were away? Some of our DVDs are missing.'

Kinley laughed. 'That was just Pemba. He watched movies almost every night. I'll ask him where they are.'

I hoped that he hadn't lost them. He probably thought they were only pirated copies, not originals worth a week of his pay each.

Kinley put up her last item and turned to me. 'Have you heard from Anna?'

Here it comes, I thought. Tell us how much you preferred Anna. 'No. I don't think Dominique's heard from her in months.'

'That's a shame. I'd love to hear what she's up to now. She used to have dinner with us all the time.'

'What do you want for dinner?'

Dominique looked up from her laptop. 'I don't know. What do you feel like?'

'Chilli con carne.'

'You're getting predictable. Can you get started? I'll join you once my email's finished downloading.'

Paprika followed me, yowling all the way and made a show of turning his nose up at the rice in his bowl.

'No more fish until you finish the rice. If you're really hungry for meat, go and catch a rat. Or have you killed them all already?'

Paprika stuck his head in the fridge as soon as I'd opened the door wide enough. Sometimes I wondered if he wasn't really a dog.

'So, what have we got here? Carrots, broccoli, ferns, chillies. Looks like it's rice and veggies again, Paprika. Be thankful you get fish every day.'

But he just yowled when I closed the door without taking out the tin of fish.

A happy squeal came down the corridor while I was putting the veggies on the bench. I just had time to turn towards the door before Dominique jumped, landing with her legs around my waist and her arms around my neck.

'I got it. I got the extension. We can stay another year.'

'That's great,' I said, spinning her around. 'I guess I need to find an income somehow, then.'

'What about the idea you had for your own company?'

'I'd need a permanent internet connection for that. We'd have to move into town.'

'Great. Then I wouldn't have to come home early from the bar when you get tired.'

'I'll start looking for a place tomorrow.'

Dominique beat her heels against my thighs and squealed in my ear.

Our landlord walked into the room and stopped, surprise showing faintly on his stern face.

I tensed, unsure how he'd feel about finding me in his bedroom.

'Murray's helping me clean all the viruses off the computer,' Pemba explained to his father. 'You know how slowly it was running.'

Kinga nodded and began changing out of his *gho*. I turned back to watch the computer finish its second scan, now showing the computer to be clean.

'I think you'll find that's much better,' I said, getting up when it was finally done.

'Oh, it is. I can see it already,' said Pemba, following me out. 'Thanks so much. Will you stay and have some dinner?'

I almost tripped down the first step. I was finally being invited to dinner casually and Dominique wasn't here to experience it. 'Are you sure?'

'Of course. There's always plenty of food.'

I followed him into the warmth of the kitchen. Small enough to only need a single window, the room had a counter running down one wall supporting a sink and a gas stove. Kinley was taking a pot of rice off the *bukari* wood stove that sat in the centre of the room.

'Hi, Murray. Are you joining us for dinner? Come in, come in. Is Dominique still away?'

Kinga sat in the corner watching television with his legs stretched out along the bench. Kinley shooed his legs away so that I could sit too. She and Pemba sat on the floor.

'Yes, she's in Samtse,' I said.

Kinley seemed impressed. 'I didn't think that *chilips* were allowed down there.'

'Apparently they opened it a few months ago for official visits only. Her colleagues think that she might be the first *chilip* ever to go to these villages.'

Kinga, more relaxed than I'd ever seen him, joined the conversation. 'She'll love it in the south. It's still very traditional. Except Phuentsholing, of course. It's too big.'

'Have you spent much time in the south?'

'I was chief magistrate in Gelephu.'

'Chief magistrate?' Pemba rolled onto his back, laughing. '*Dasho* Kinga.'

A smile threatened to appear on Kinga's face as Kinley joined the laughter, also teasing him about his lost title.

'Why did you come back?'

'I wanted to give my children a better education. For all the good it's done them, I might as well have stayed. No respect for their elders.'

Kinley handed me a plate of rice and *ema datshi* and the casual conversation continued while we ate.

'Where's your other daughter?'

'Sangay? Right now, she's in India, doing a special ritual. She has to prostrate one hundred and eleven thousand, one hundred and eleven times.'

'The full thing?' I tried to imagine moving between standing up and lying down so many times. 'That must take months.'

'About two months. You can only manage about a few hundred on the first day, but your body gets stronger quickly. Then you can do many thousands per day.' Kinley sounded like she was talking from experience.

'Have you done it?'

She carried more weight than most Bhutanese women, along with all the jolliness of the innkeeper stereotype. 'Yes. I did it a few years ago.'

'What do you get out of it?' A few answers ran through my head. Enlightenment, fitness, better concentration.

'Ah, because you do so much exercise, you can eat as much as you like. And monks are great cooks.'

I couldn't help but laugh and Kinley joined me.

'I've got to get back to finish up some work,' I said when dinner was over, familiar with the ritual. 'Thank you so much for the delicious meal.'

'I'm glad you came,' Kinley said. 'Anna used to come and eat with us all the time, you know.'

As I closed the door behind me, I understood. Every week we'd been told that Anna used to be part of the family and every week we took offence that we hadn't been invited to do the same. In fact, they mentioned Anna as a subtle rebuke that we weren't sharing our lives with them as much as Anna had. It was up to us to invite ourselves to dinner.

My grimace at the irony of understanding too late turned to a grimace at the squeal of our cat as I entered our flat.

Michael pulled up in their Maruti while I was squeezing the last items of a load into our own car.

'Where's May?' I asked. 'Couldn't she make it?'

'No. She wanted to tell you herself, but the timing's wrong. We're pregnant.'

'Congratulations.' I held out my hand to shake his. 'When did this happen?'

'She's just gone into the second trimester. We've been trying for a few years now, so we didn't want to tell anyone until we were sure.'

'Was it the relaxed atmosphere of Bhutan that made the difference?'

Michael had a guilty expression as he laughed. 'Funny you should ask. We thought that might help, but we weren't having any luck here either so we decided to try Chimi Lakhang, that temple on the way to Punakha.'

'The one that's meant to help with fertility? Don't tell me you've become superstitious.'

'We're not, but it couldn't hurt, right?'

'I guess not. What happened?'

I leant on our car, looking across the valley at the first tinges of green appearing amongst the vegetation. Beside me, Michael leant back too. I wondered if he was looking at the same thing, but then he responded to my question.

'We went through the usual ritual, then the monk donged us both on the head with a wooden phallus like they do at the *tsetchu*. A week later, May was pregnant.'

'Surely you don't believe...'

'I wouldn't say I believe, but it does make you wonder. How many times since you got here have you heard of things occurring that match the superstition?' He looked around. 'Couldn't you get the truck?'

The director of RIM had offered us the RIM ute and a driver to move all our stuff into town.

'I don't know. It was meant to be here by now.'

'I hope it comes. The director might have forgotten to tell the driver and even if he did, the man might be sleeping in.'

'Well, the director gave me his home number in case of real problems. If they don't come soon, I'll call.' As I finished speaking, we heard the sound of an engine struggling up the driveway. 'This must be them. Do you want to tell Dominique the news? She's inside cleaning.'

I watched the driver and his friend heave a mattress onto the truck. It would have been tough without them. We were going to have to make a second trip with all three vehicles. How had we managed to accumulate so much in just a year?

Michael got his car started while I went to talk to the truckies. Dominique had gone on ahead.

'You'll follow us, right?'

The driver nodded, then dropped his voice to a whisper. 'Is that... Is that Michael from *Druk Ge Goem?*'

I couldn't help laughing at their awe of an ordinary man. 'Yes. That's him.'

'Wow. Thank you for asking us to help today. Now I have something to tell my friends.'

I was still laughing when I got in the car.

'What's so funny?'

'They're in awe of you. You're Michael from *Druk Ge Goem.*'

'I thought that might be it. I refuse to walk into town since they put that massive sign up over the theatre. Wherever I go, people stare and point at me.'

My mobile rang as he drove off. I recognised the number as the internet company.

'Is this Mr. Murray Gunn?'

'It is. We're on our way to the new flat now. Can you join us?'

'I'm sorry, Mr. Murray, sir. I'm calling to tell you that we don't have the power supply for the antenna.'

'What's wrong?' asked Michael when he saw my face.

I waved him to silence. 'But I gave you a month's notice. You said you had everything.'

'I know, sir. I'm sorry, sir, but the last customer didn't return the power supply.'

'When can you get a new one?'

'We'll order it today, sir. I expect it to arrive in two or three weeks.'

'Do you realise we're moving into town solely so we can get better internet access? That's why I gave you so much notice.'

'I'm sorry, sir.'

'When do they say they can get the parts?' asked Michael when I'd hung up.

'Two weeks.'

'So, a month or two, then. What are you going to do?'

'I'll have to try the new company. They only offer "better than dial-up," but it might be enough.'

'I hate to say it, but it serves you right for choosing a black day to move house.'

We sat in silence for the rest of the drive.

A couple of kids were playing in the building's parking lot when we arrived. Their mouths became round when we got out of the car. One of them went running inside, shouting, 'Mum, Mum, it's Michael!'

'Shit.' He looked at me. 'And don't you laugh. You were almost in this situation yourself.'

For the first time, I was extremely glad that it hadn't been me.

'Michael!'

'Michael!'

I couldn't help laughing at Michael's reactions to the shouts. Every inch of him failed to be a movie star. Shoulders hunched, he looked straight ahead, expression fixed.

'Is this really the first time you've walked into town since the poster went up?'

'I even have to threaten him just so he'll go to the local shops.' May was enjoying Michael's discomfort almost as much as I was.

'It's not just the sign. It's the interviews for the television, radio and the newspaper. I can't go anywhere or do anything without seeing my face and hearing my name. How would you like it?'

'You're right. I probably wouldn't. I'm so glad it was you.'

The expat extras were all waiting outside the theatre under a ten-metre-long picture of Michael, Dorji Wangmo and a couple of yaks. Around them were a few hundred Bhutanese, all waiting to see the star at his premiere.

'Come on. Let's go in,' he said after allowing us all to take pictures of him in front of the poster.

Dorji Wangmo and Kinley Dorji were waiting inside and directed us to our seats at the front of the mezzanine. As we sat down, everyone on the floor below turned to look up and whisper. We all knew that they only had eyes for Michael.

When the theatre was full, Kinley Dorji turned on the portable projector sitting on the balustrade in front of him and pressed play.

The movie starts with us all arriving at the airport, Michael in a suit to stand out, and having lunch in a hotel. Then Michael is silly enough to get separated from the group on a trek. In the dark, he panics and runs, falling and hurting his knee. While the army is out looking for him, he is found by a beautiful yak herder who carries him back to her tent. Plenty of language jokes ensue as they try to communicate. When the yak herder's sister turns up, she is able to translate, but they don't want to let anyone know he is there because it would ruin the yak herder's reputation and her chance of ever finding a man. However, they do find a doctor who is able to twist his knee back into place and over the weeks Michael's strength recovers.

One day when they're alone, Michael says 'I love you.' '*Lafu?*' she asks, confused, but dutifully rummages round for a turnip. From that moment, the movie becomes a musical as they sing their love to each other. Eventually, the officials track Michael down and drag him back to Thimphu so they can send him home. The yak herder and her sister follow and beg the government to let him stay. They get a couple of days together, managing to dress Michael up in a *gho* and take him to the king's birthday celebrations before he's put on a plane. In the final scene, Michael returns for a wedding in Laya.

The lights came back on and almost a thousand people stood up and turned to cheer Michael. They waited at the bottom of the stairs to shake his hand as we came down. Dorji Wangmo seemed forgotten in all the fuss.

'Come on. Let's get out of here,' said Michael when he finally managed to join us outside. 'Dinner's on me at Centrepoint.'

A feast of Japanese and Bhutanese food was laid out on long tables. After the two-and-a-half-hour movie, we were all famished and began eating immediately.

'Michael,' I said when I could get his attention. 'You did an amazing job. I once thought I'd be a better actor than you, but I couldn't have done nearly as well.'

Michael laughed. 'I knew that I couldn't act, so I didn't try. Luckily, I was playing a foreigner lost and confused in Bhutan, so I could just be myself.'

'What about the singing?'

We all knew that he'd mimed most songs to the voice of one of our Bhutanese friends, but the wedding scene was his own voice and in Dzongkha.

'I had to learn all that, and we did it line by line. It took forever. The funny thing, though, is that last scene wasn't meant to be in the movie. It originally stopped when I got sent home, but the censorship board wouldn't let it go out like that. They said that Bhutanese wanted to see happy, colourful films like Bollywood and the ending was too sad, so we had to shoot another scene where I came back.'

'Yeshey, what happened in 1990 with the Southern Bhutanese?'

I was sitting at my new desk in his office, where I'd set up to help him pay the rent and continue cultural contact now that I wasn't teaching at

RIM. His Southern Bhutanese staff were travelling around the country installing the new government network.

'When we stopped the rebellion, you mean?'

'Is that what happened? No one will talk about it.' But Yeshey had become a good friend and I hoped he'd at least tell the Bhutanese side of the story.

'The Southern Bhutanese were plotting to overthrow the king. They're a very smart and determined people and they wanted to rule the country, to make it a democracy immediately. But our king is smart too and he found out about the plot and arrested the ringleaders.'

'But there are one hundred thousand refugees.'

'Most of them fled because they were involved in the conspiracy and didn't want to be arrested. Some were told to leave because they refused to obey the new laws.'

'What were the new laws?'

'That everyone had to wear traditional dress in public. That everyone had to speak Dzongkha in official places. The Code of Conduct.'

'I've never seen it, but it does seem extremely strict. It's too hot in Southern Bhutan to wear the *gho*. No wonder they refused.'

'You get used to the heat, but the laws are important to ensure our national identity continues. Bhutan doesn't want to be swallowed up like Tibet, Sikkim or Assam. China and India took over those countries using the excuse that they were culturally the same. The Code of Conduct was made to stop that happening to Bhutan. But we don't want to be like Nepal, either. That's why the king is being so careful about introducing the constitution.'

'Do you think it's the right move?'

'I do, as long as the king retains the power to overrule the government. But most Bhutanese want to keep it the way it is. They're scared that the Southern Bhutanese will take control.'

I paused, wondering how far I dared push the topic. 'Would that be so bad? You've said that they're smart and determined.'

'And generally better educated too, but you can't really trust them. They're out for themselves and they'll steal.'

'How can you employ Southern Bhutanese if you believe that?'

Yeshey laughed. 'I've got lots of Southern Bhutanese friends and we always joke about this. They just laugh and agree when we say that you can't trust them. Some of my Bhutanese friends are more racist. They often warn me to be careful with Raj and Hari because they'll try to steal my money, but Raj is the best engineer I know. Why would I employ someone who wasn't as good?'

I walked into Bhutan International, HP's local distributor, with a laptop I'd bought in India and waited for service. When no one appeared at the reception desk after five minutes, I poked my head through the door that said 'staff only.'

'Yes, sir. Can I help you?'

'I've got a problem with this laptop. It looks like the BIOS is dead.'

He turned it over, obviously not recognising the advanced model. 'Did you buy it here?'

'No, so I didn't want to bother you with it, but when I called the help desk in Singapore, they said it would be best for you to send it to them through the normal channels.'

He was looking a bit confused. If you want it done right, best to do it yourself and leave as little to them as possible.

'Here's the name of the person I spoke to and the ticket they opened. They have the power supply and everything. All you have to do is send the laptop itself.'

'Okay, sir.'

'When do you think it will be ready? How long does it normally take?'

He thought for a few seconds. 'Hmmm. I can send it today and it usually takes about two weeks.'

'Fine. Do I need to pay for shipping?'

'I don't know. We'll call you if you do.'

Dr. Norbu sat across from me, bouncing his shoulders and grinning *doma* as usual. 'I'm so glad that you and Dominique could stay.' Shoulder bounce. 'We have so much to do this year.'

Dominique came out from the next room where she and the other girls from the office had been playing with the new baby of her colleague. As she snuggled up beside me, I caught a cheeky grin that said 'this ought to be good.'

I decided to nudge the show along. 'What do you have planned? Are you still trying to produce more milk?'

Dominique hadn't given up trying to build the brand image of Bhutanese cheese in India to cope with the additional production urged by her department. This work had prompted her to start asking the hard questions, like what their goals were and why she was developing the database.

'Oh yes. More milk. Better milk. We're the livestock department. We need to improve the milk output.'

'The database must still be important, then.'

Shoulder bounce. Giggle. 'Of course. We need the database to track the breeding program. Dominique's work is very important.'

'But Dominique's not an IT person. You really need someone with database skills to design it properly.'

'Yes, yes. I've made the request. They're coming.'

'When?'

'Maybe next month.' He'd been telling Dominique the same thing for almost a year.

'Great. So, you're going to increase the milk by breeding better. What else will you do? What's the vision for the Department of Livestock? What do you want to achieve?'

This was what Dominique was waiting for. She'd told me that Dr. Norbu was a good veterinarian, probably a great one, but it was clear he wasn't meant for leadership. Now, in his relaxed state, we both hoped to see his limits, his aspirations.

'I think we should put our efforts into embryo transfer of a yak.'

I was stunned beyond my expectations. Unless I'd missed something, he would waste good people on work that had no economic benefit. 'What for? Do you want to bring yaks into the breeding program? Is their milk good enough to worry about?'

'Not really, but no one's ever transferred the embryo of a yak. Bhutan could be the first.'

Dominique was working at home when I got back from Yeshey's office.

I kissed her ear and got a grunt in return. 'What's up?'

She swivelled her chair slowly, remaining slumped. 'It should have been a good day. I got permission to work on a strategy for the Department of Livestock, starting with a full evaluation of our current situation.'

'That's great. Now you can really start to show your skills and I guess you can see more of the country.'

'I still have to do the database work, but you're right, it should be a lot more interesting now.'

'So what's the downside?'

'I took our rent form in to get signed today and Dr. Norbu said, 'Oh, you've moved. This form only covers the old house."

'How long will it take them to approve the new address?' It suddenly seemed a pointless question. 'A couple of weeks, I bet.'

'He said they can't. He said that the request should have been made before we moved and now it's too late.'

'But he knew we were moving.'

'Of course he did. We talked about it a number of times over the last couple of months. I think he's angry with me for going over his head about the strategy work, so now he's acting surprised and saying that he didn't know we were moving.'

'But that's the only expense they have for all your work. Now they expect you to go to all this extra effort for nothing? Go over his head again. If you find out which department handles the rent, can't we arrange it ourselves?'

A smile flickered on her face to be replaced by doubt, but the smile returned. 'We can, can't we? We're veterans of the system now.'

I walked straight into the staff-only area of Bhutan International and found my laptop on a bench, waiting for the technician to finish his phone call.

'Yes, sir?'

'This is my laptop. I got a message from you.'

'Yes, sir.'

'Is it ready? How much do I owe?'

'It's not ready, sir. We haven't been able to do anything because you didn't leave the power supply.'

I held my breath, trying to keep my temper, but I couldn't. I found myself reaching out for the papers on the laptop. 'I gave you everything you needed. All you had to do was send the main unit to Singapore with the ticket number shown here.'

I thrust the papers in his face, but they slipped out of my hand, then dodged my every attempt to snatch them before they hit the floor. The humiliation of having lost control only fuelled my anger and was worsened by having to crouch to pick up the papers.

'You've had two weeks and you wait until now to tell me that you haven't done anything. I've been relying on you to fix it so I can go on with my business.'

'I'm sorry, sir.'

'Don't be sorry. Send the bloody thing to Singapore like you agreed to do.'

'Yes, sir. I'm sorry, sir. But did you bring the power supply?'

I was moping on the way home from work. Dominique was away again and this time she'd taken a colleague each from the marketing and livestock divisions. I was left at home to research potential customers for my company and I found that research and sales work were as troublesome as I thought they'd be.

A stray dog trotted past me, keeping its distance. Bare feet appeared in my view, followed closely by a walking stick and the red robes of a monk, ten metres ahead and approaching slowly.

Tonight would be lonely. I hadn't expected Dominique to be away so much. There was a video store on the way home – all pirated copies from Bangkok, of course. Perhaps they'd have the new Batman movie.

The dog stepped off the footpath to avoid the monk, but it wasn't quick enough. The old man lashed out with his walking stick, cracking the dog on the head and again on the back before it could jump out of reach.

I stopped, unsure I'd really seen what I thought I'd seen, while the monk put his weight back on the stick, straightened up and walked past me, muttering.

I walked into Bhutan International for the third time and found my laptop sitting in the same place.

'Is this ready yet?'

'Sir, no sir,' said the same technician, approaching cautiously. 'We need you to pay for the shipping, sir. We can't send it to Singapore until you've paid.'

I didn't even try to hold back my temper this time. I stalked out of the workshop and into the manager's office. 'What kind of operation are you running here?'

She looked up at me, to the technician who'd followed, then back at me again. 'What's the problem, sir?'

'He hasn't paid the shipping fee,' said the technician, 'so we couldn't send his laptop to Singapore.'

'Ah, yes. You'll need to pay three thousand ngultrum for the shipping, sir.'

'Why couldn't you have told me that five weeks ago? I gave you everything you needed then. I even asked if I'd need to pay for shipping and said I was prepared for that.'

'But you didn't—'

'I gave my contact details so that you could contact me if it did turn out that I needed to pay something. I just need my laptop fixed.'

'I'm sorry, sir. If you pay the money now, we'll send it today.'

'Your technicians have told me that twice already. I don't trust you any more. I'll send it myself.' I began to move away, but suddenly I had more to say. 'This kind of service might be acceptable for your Bhutanese customers, who are all pretty relaxed and have their own relaxed customers, but it won't work in the international market.'

The woman's blank stare didn't flicker.

'How can you call your company "international" if you aren't ready to work in the real world? What happens when Bhutan has call centres servicing international customers? They won't be as forgiving as I've been. If you want to have them come to you for equipment and service, you'll need to do a lot better than you've done for me.'

'I'm sorry, sir.'

Yeshey's office faced south. From my desk, where I'd just finished the first component of the inventory system, I could only see a swathe of green where a ridge curled into view of the indented arch windows. I went to stand in front of Yeshey's desk to get the full panorama. High up to the right was the Nose where we went rock climbing most Sundays. Straight ahead was the *lakhang*, perched on the hill at Babesa where we used to live. To the left, past the river, was the road out of town, winding back to Paro and the turn off to Punakha in the east.

As I watched, a string of Toyota Prados made its way along the road towards town. On the streets below, everybody in view stopped to watch the procession.

'The royal entourage is bigger than usual today,' I said. 'Is it the king? Is that why everyone's watching?'

Yeshey looked up from his computer where he was putting together a proposal to provide the network and fifty computers for a new call centre. If Bhutan International showed the dedication he did, I'd have had my laptop back weeks ago.

'It's not the king,' he said. 'It's the Je Kempo.'

'The head lama? Why does he need such a grand procession?' Then I understood. 'Today is the first day of summer.'

Yeshey grinned as he nodded. 'That's right. I hope you're not wearing thermals today.'

On the first day of summer, the main monk body moved from the tropics of Punakha back to Thimphu and while they were there, it was forbidden to wear thermals.

I lifted the hem of my *gho* to flash my leg. As Kinga used to say, Bhutan is one of the few countries where the men show their bare legs and the women hide theirs.

'It's not cold enough for thermals any more,' I said. 'But how did you know that they were coming back today? I didn't see anything in the paper, but it looks like everyone else in town knew.'

'No. It's never announced, and was probably only decided this morning, but Bhutan is a small country. Some of the younger monks would have told their families that they were coming back. Those people would have told their cousins and they would have told their cousins. Pretty soon, everybody knows.'

Two taxis pulled up next to me. The drivers got out and looked at my two wardrobes standing at the edge of a road surrounded by rice fields. The first driver raised his eyebrows and wiped sweat from his forehead while the second asked where I was taking them.

'Changangkha,' I told him, naming our new suburb.

The carpenter who'd built them left his shack to help tie the wardrobes to the roof of the taxis. Then he threw some planks of wood I'd ordered for shelves into the back, grunted and returned to his workshop. It had been a fight every step of the way. He was Indian and spoke almost no English, but I'd made my order through one of the furniture shops in town. Bhutanese don't much go for clothes that hang so I'd had to design the wardrobes myself.

I enjoyed doing that and he'd given me a good price, but kept delaying the date. 'Come back next week and we'll see.'

Eventually I'd threatened to take my business elsewhere if the order wasn't ready by the following week. Then yesterday he'd promised he'd deliver them this morning if I met him at the shop to direct him home. At the shop, he'd said that they were at his workshop outside town. When we reached the workshop, he'd called his friend to make the delivery only to find that his friend was on a run to Paro.

I had pointed at my watch to ask how long he'd be, but the carpenter had shrugged. Paro was an hour and a half away. I could waste hours sitting there waiting, hours that I could be using to research potential clients.

He made it clear that he didn't like it, but he called two other taxis to help instead. Now that they'd arrived, he was making it equally clear that if I wasn't going to use his friend's taxi, he wasn't going to help me get them into our flat.

No matter. Someone would be around.

But the car park was empty when we arrived and no one turned up during the time it took to unload everything. I really didn't like to leave them out in the open until a neighbour returned from work.

'Which floor?' asked the vocal driver.

'Third.'

They each picked up an end of one of the wardrobes and moved towards the entrance.

'Are you sure you've got time?' I asked.

'Of course,' he said with a laugh. 'In Bhutan, everyone has time.'

Madeleine pulled open the door to the shack and called out, 'Are you open?'

A reply bounced back from the darkness and Madeleine beckoned me to follow her inside. I locked the bikes together against the wall of the restaurant and joined her. Madeleine had borrowed Dominique's bike and we'd ridden to Hongtsho for breakfast. Hongtsho, a thousand metres above the capital, was a settlement of Tibetan refugees that marked the eastern border of Thimphu Dzongkhag. This was the limit of the free access zone for non-Bhutanese.

'I ordered you *thukpa*, Murray. It's a Tibetan soup and dumplings and it's the shop speciality. I hope you're okay with that.'

I nodded as I slid onto the bench across from her, feeling the tension ease from my legs. I'd done the ride up this mountain a number of times, but it never seemed to get any easier.

'Dominique gets back today, doesn't she?' asked Madeleine. 'You must be excited.'

We hadn't had much time to talk on the two-hour ride up. All our energy had gone into pedalling and when we stopped to catch our breath, our attention had been on the view. At every corner, the fresh green of the trees stretched up and down the valley to the next corner and beyond. The chill morning air sat still on our cheeks and the forest was silent. I missed the bird calls, ever present in the forests of Australia, but their lack intensified Bhutan's feeling of isolation. City life felt more distant here than in any of my favourite hiking spots in the Blue Mountains.

'Definitely,' I said. 'It seems longer than three weeks. I've kept myself busy, ordering wardrobes, putting up shelves and tidying the place so it doesn't look like we're camping any more.'

The owner placed our breakfast in front of us.

'I've also filled the drinking water dispenser and got her bike fixed. When we get back this morning, I'll make a trip to the market to stock up the fridge. She's not going to come home this time and say that our house looks like a bachelor's flat.'

'It sounds like you're really fixing the place up,' said Madeleine, scooping a dumpling.

I took a sip of the soup and winced at the bitterness. 'I guess I am, but we're expecting this to be our home for a few more years.'

'Well, I'm sure she won't complain this time. She'll probably drag you straight off to bed.' Madeleine was slurping down her soup with a gusto I couldn't match, apparently enjoying the bitter taste.

'I'm counting on it. Three weeks is a long time.'

'Hello stranger,' called a voice from the bedroom.

I dropped the shopping and went in to find Dominique sitting at her computer with her back to me.

'You're early. I wasn't expecting you back until this evening.' I wanted to pick her up and swing her around, but she stayed seated so I hugged her from behind and kissed her neck, making her squirm. 'How was the trip?'

She turned to face me. 'It was amazing. Sonam and Wangchuk are great to travel with.'

'Wangchuk?'

The colleague who'd kissed her. The one who'd said his offer would stand whenever she wished to take it up.

'It's fine, Murray. We're getting along really well again, now.'

That wasn't exactly comforting, but Dominique would only get upset if I raised my concern. 'How are you feeling? Do you want to go for a walk?'

'Maybe later.' She turned back to the laptop. 'I have a lot of work to do. I have to get all my ideas down while I still remember them.'

Yeshey was on the phone when I arrived at the office. From the one-sided conversation, I understood that his van had been stolen.

'What happened?' I asked when he got off the call, and only then noticed the bags under his eyes.

'I was working late last night. When I left at about nine o'clock I found a bunch of teenagers sticking something into the lock of the building manager's car.'

I tried to imagine what I'd have done in that situation. Would I have had the courage to confront them?

'I told them off. They stood around looking ashamed while I asked which school they went to and whether this was conduct that the school would condone. Eventually I told them to leave quickly or I'd call the police. I didn't notice that my van was missing until they'd gone.'

'Shit. And you just had them in hand?'

'There's no way to be sure. I couldn't prove that they were actually trying to break the lock, even if I could recognise them again. It's embarrassing. We like to brag about how peaceful Bhutan is, but then things like this happen.'

'What are you going to do?' The van would have been almost a year's savings for Yeshey.

'The friend I was just talking to has a spare van that he's willing to lend me so that my staff can get around to finish setting up the network in each *dzongkhag*, but I still hope to find my own van.'

'I'm sorry, Yeshey. Is there any way I can help?'

'I don't think so. I already drove down every road in Thimphu last night and the police are looking for it too. There aren't many places to hide a car in this country, so it'll have to turn up soon.'

Dominique was at her computer when I got home, which meant she'd probably been in town at the marketing division again. Meeting with him.

She didn't get up when I went in to say hello, but then she hadn't gotten up to greet me in the few days since she came home. I recognised the music she had playing on her laptop. 'Are you listening to Rokia Traore?'

Dominique had gone to see her in concert in the weeks between the time we met and our first date. The complex rhythms and strong, pure voice always brought back memories of courting.

'Yeah. I don't think I told you that I was playing this on the iPod when we were travelling.' She began to laugh and I smiled at the sound. 'The others asked what I was listening to, so I let them hear it. You know what they said?'

I shook my head.

'Wangchuk said "I didn't realise that African music was so backward. They could learn from Bhutanese musicians."'

I tried to laugh at the irony of Wangchuk's comment, but I was getting tired of hearing Dominique talk happily about this man who'd kissed her.

'It's so good to work with him. He really understands what I'm trying to do.'

There was no point in getting jealous. It wasn't as if anything could have happened on the trip. There were three of them and they stayed in farmhouses every night. Not that the lack of privacy would necessarily have stopped Wangchuk. If the night hunting legends were true, he'd probably had sex with girls while her parents slept in the same room. But Dominique was too shy to let that happen, even if she did like him.

I ran a finger down the side of her neck and down her arm, grabbing her hand firmly and guiding it away from the keyboard. She'd been working until after I went to bed every night for the past week, then getting up grumpy every morning. It was time to distract her.

She pulled her hand roughly out of my grip. 'Not now, Murray. I've got lots of work to do.'

It was still early, so I didn't meet anyone until I stepped out the front door and into the rain. There stood the woman whose children had been so excited to see Michael. Laid out beside her were six plastic containers, each set beneath a drip falling from the roof five storeys up.

'Still no water?' I asked.

She shook her head and kicked one of her containers out of the way to make room for mine. 'The tank is dry.'

The drip moved as soon as I put the saucepan down. It soon settled, but the pot would take a long time to fill.

I'd secretly prayed for a blackout so I could pry Dominique away from writing her report. Such power cuts in Babesa had disrupted our routine, but I now realised that it had been a minor sacrifice compared to loss of water. At least we'd been able to cook with gas and use candles for light. And there had been ways to pass the evening when we couldn't use our computers.

This was the third day with no water and I was coming to understand how much we took it for granted. We could buy drinking water, but it was expensive to cook with and impossible to shower with. I hadn't realised how often I washed my hands until the tank dried up. Or perhaps I caught myself trying to wash them so often only because they were never clean any more. But the worst problem was the inability to flush the toilet. We'd each had to resort to the public toilets at our respective workplaces. Today we'd have to ask friends if we could use their showers.

Poor Selden, I thought. Dominique's colleague lived in government housing and had to carry all her family's water up two storeys because the pressure was only enough to reach the ground floor.

'Is the landlord getting it fixed?' I'd asked the same question yesterday and the day before.

Her shrug said it all. The landlord was probably maintaining that the problem was with the town supply and there was nothing he could do about it. He refused to see that if our neighbours all had water, it was more likely to be a problem in the building's pipes.

'He's got to do something. If it wasn't raining, we'd be in even bigger trouble.'

She sighed and began picking up her pots. 'What to do, *la?*'

I grabbed the nearly full saucepan and carried it carefully back to our flat. Dominique would be up soon and I wanted to boil some water for her coffee. Nothing mattered to me more than our relationship. As much as I loved this country and its people, there would be no reason for me to be here without her. The same went for my business. I was determined to put every effort into making her happy. If that meant supporting her while she did the report and staying in the background until it was done, I'd manage.

Dominique came out of the bedroom as I ducked into the kitchen. She saw the pot and swore. '*Putain!* Still no water?'

'Did you have trouble sleeping again?' I asked as I poured the water into the boiler.

When the reply didn't come, I sneaked off to my study.

As soon as the monsoon deluge had stopped, Madeleine and I decided to meet up for dinner. Dominique declined to join us, claiming she still needed to work on her report, so I walked down the hill alone.

The rain for the last hour had been so heavy that water wouldn't have been a problem for a couple of days even if our pipes hadn't started flowing again. At the insistence of every resident in the block, the landlord had finally called in a plumber to fix the supply problem. I'd put a few containers out to collect water anyway, just in case.

Our street ran along the contour of the hill and with no gutters, the rain had washed dirt onto the road. The metre-wide drains that ran under the street and down the hill were still full and flowing fast. I turned downhill along a road which snaked across the steep descent. Piles of dirt had collected at the corners. Much higher, I thought, and they'd be a BMX biker's dream berms.

I stopped short at the next intersection which was at least ankle-deep in water. This river, helped by the concave Bhutanese roads, was at the top of a hill and spilling down the next road like an overflowing dam. I looked for a way to cross and saw a large stone block sitting in the middle of the road. It was more than two feet on each edge and was in the direct flow of the drain, probably washed out of position by the monsoon. I marvelled at the force required to push it a couple of metres into the middle of the road.

And this, according to the locals, was the dying gasp of a monsoon that had already raged across India, exhausting itself on the way.

Madeleine had come to pick up Dominique for a game of tennis. 'Is Murray going to join us?' she asked when she arrived.

I poked my head into the living room.

'I'd love to, Madeleine, but Dominique said there weren't enough rackets.'

'I'm sure we'd manage, even if we had to take turns.'

Dominique glared at me. 'Can't I even play tennis with my friends without you interfering?'

Madeleine paled. 'I'll just wait outside.'

'Dominique, I like tennis too,' I said, when the door had closed behind Madeleine. 'And they're not just your friends. They're ours.'

'But why do we have to do everything together? I need some time to myself.'

'We don't do anything together any more, except eat breakfast and you're usually so grumpy then that I can't talk to you. You're almost always travelling and when you're here, you're working.'

'We do so do things together. You always ride beside me when I go running.'

'And how much do you talk to me then? You won't let me join *taikwondo* and you never come to climbing. You won't even give me a hug goodnight any more. It's not the sort of quality time I expect from a relationship.'

Dominique sighed. 'You're just always so unhappy, now. Why would I want to spend more time with you?'

I felt my fists clench and forced myself to relax them. 'How happy would you be if the person you married refused to touch you or even to show interest in you? You always find ways for us to be apart.'

'You should find your own activities to do, too.'

'Fuck, Dominique,' I said, kicking the sofa bench hard. Pain shot through my toes. I'd forgotten my feet were bare. Dominique didn't notice me wince. She barely seemed to register my existence as she went about getting ready. I was as much a ghost to her as she was to me. 'I'm talking about our relationship. I've given up my life so you can build your career, but you don't seem to appreciate that. You don't seem to care what I feel at all.'

'Why don't you stop moping and try to join an archery squad or start a writing group? You're always talking about how much you miss the one in Brussels.'

'That would be great, wouldn't it? And if we slept in different rooms, we'd never have to see each other at all. It's like you want a flatmate, not a husband.'

She rounded on me. 'And you don't want a wife. You want a dog.'

Sangay Wangchuk leaned back in his director's chair and smiled, his lips stained with *doma*.

'How are things in DIT these days, Sangay?' I asked.

'Busy, busy. It's always so busy.'

I suppressed a smirk. He was never too busy to let me leave without a leisurely cup of butter tea.

'And you, Mr. Murray? How's your business?'

'It's very slow, Sangay. I've been talking to each of the development organisations here and they obviously need my help. They spend a lot of money on travel that takes their staff away from their posts for days at a time, and they don't communicate well with their international offices. But they resist the idea of putting time into setting up a better solution.'

'Ah, it's always that way. Everyone's so busy.'

'It's not just being busy. Even the organisations that get excited by the idea have valid reasons why it will be better to start in a couple of months – after they've upgraded their network or once the new IT position has been filled. The others just don't think it's possible to communicate effectively over distance.'

Sangay leaned forward, his tone conspiratorial. 'You should tell them about Lhuntse.'

I leaned in to catch his words. 'What happened in Lhuntse?'

'Our people just put in the wireless phone system last week.'

'Really? Isn't that Bhutan Telecom's job?'

'Yes, but they were only going to put in ten lines and there are three or four hundred households and many of them are far away, so DIT stepped in. We used Bhutan Telecom's satellite connection out to the centre of the village and put in a small phone system there. Now there are about fifty phones scattered through the village.'

'Wow. That must be really exciting for them.'

'Of course. Now they can easily call back to Thimphu and they can make local calls for one ngultrum. But the real story happened during the installation. My team were in one of the most remote houses setting up the phone with a solar power battery when the old man that lived there got really sick.'

'Was it serious?'

'Very.'

His expression gave the word such exaggerated gravity that I had to hold back a perverse urge to laugh.

'He told my team that all his family were out visiting. His wife was at her friend's house on the other side of the village a few hours' walk away. They had just installed a phone in that same house, so they called her. She returned with more friends and they carried him to the basic health unit.'

'Lucky for him.'

'Very lucky. They say he might have died if he'd had to wait for her to come home the next day.'

Sangay had made himself another *doma* package to chew as soon as he'd finished his butter tea and as it numbed his lips he started to slur more than usual.

'Have you heard about the new call shentre, Mr. Murray?'

I nodded. 'Yeshey has talked about it. He's bidding on the computer and network part of it, I think.'

'Yes. I heard that, too. Have you ever had anything to do with call centres?'

'I have set up a few in my time. They're probably the most interesting aspect of phone systems.' I picked up my tea and found it still too hot to drink.

'Perhaps you can help me. I'm worried about whether my team can handle the call centre. We've never had to set one up before.'

His slurring was getting worse by the minute and I was already having trouble following his words. 'I'm sure that won't be a problem. You've got lots of capable people and the technology's not that difficult. The tricky part of call centres is keeping the morale of the staff up.'

He leaned forward with interest, forehead creased and lips slack. 'Why's that?'

I took a sip and scalded my tongue. 'Because they have to deal with lots of angry customers and it will be worse here because you've got a strong accent.'

'Why would that matter? We speak good English.'

'You do, but your customers are going to be people from Australia and America and they want to talk to someone who knows their local environment. When they call up for concert tickets, they expect that the person selling them knows how to get to the venue. When they call to complain about their internet service, they expect that the person at the other end of the phone has used that same service. If the person you're talking to has an accent, it's clear that he's in a different country and doesn't really understand your needs.'

Sangay sat back in his chair, deep in thought. I was about to speak again when he leaned forward, eyes wide.

'We'd better make shure we don't hire anyone that chewsh *doma*, then.'

I'd never seen Yeshey angry, but the way he slammed the office door open made it clear he was today. He threw a large envelope onto his desk and sat down heavily. It looked like one of the local hand-made types that cost twice the price of the imported factory-made kind.

'What's wrong, Yeshey?' I asked, looking at the envelope. 'Is that news on your van?'

It had been missing for weeks now and we'd lost all hope. We realised that it would have been easy enough to swap the plates on it and get it past the checkpoints and even easier to get it into India.

'No. The van's gone now. It's these government regulations. They make no sense.'

I wasn't sure whether to laugh or feel sorry for him. It was great to know that locals could find the bureaucracy as tiresome as me, but if he was learning from my attitude, I wasn't doing him any favours.

'Which regulations are these?'

'Tenders. You remember that tender I was working on a few weeks ago?'

I got up and moved to the seat across from his desk, nodding as I went.

'Well, they knocked it back.'

'They probably had a better offer, Yeshey. You can't let that upset you. You just need to find out why the other bid won and try to beat them next time on those grounds.'

'I asked why. There wasn't another bid. Mine was the only one.'

I recoiled in shock. 'Why would they refuse it, then?'

'Because they have to. Legally, they can't accept a tender without at least two competitive bids.' He picked up the envelope and tipped out some stamps. 'I paid one-and-a-half thousand ngultrum just for the details document.' That was as much as I gave him in rent each month, a large sum of money in Bhutan. 'Then I have to pay for official stamps to say that I have the right to tender.'

I'd seen the rest. The weeks of work researching and documenting the proposal, the careful binding, the sealing of the envelope with a particular red wax and the pressing of a one-ngultrum coin to mark the seal. It had seemed a lot of effort to go to when he could have just walked up the street and put it on Sangay's desk, but protocol had to be followed if he wanted the business.

'So what happens now? Will they drop the work?'

Yeshey steepled his fingers. 'No. It needs to be done, so they're reopening the tender. I'll just have to convince some of my competitors to apply as well this time. It's ironic, isn't it?'

'At least you don't have to put in all that work again.'

'But I do. I have to go through the whole process for a second time, including paying for the details document and checking that nothing has changed in the request. It's not much less work than last time.'

'Sir, we need help too.'

I walked over to see what Deki Wangmo and her friend were working on. Each group had their own project to meet real needs of real organisations. Most of them had chosen other technologies, but a few were using the ones I'd been helping them learn. Deki grabbed me when I'd dropped by to discuss progress on the inventory system with Kuenga.

'Sir, this should be returning the total cost, but it's just showing the first item.'

'Okay,' I said. 'Show me the code that generates the number.'

I scanned the section Deki pointed to. 'Did you write this?'

She paused, obviously debating whether that would be a good thing or not. Finally, she shook her head. 'Tshering Dorji wrote it, sir.'

'I'm afraid you're going to have to ask him, Deki. This code is way above my level. I don't even recognise half of these constructs.'

'We can't ask him, sir. You know what he's like.'

I had to admit that I wasn't familiar with the name.

'That's not surprising, sir. He never talks to anyone. He's not very good with people. Just with computers. He knows how to do everything, but doesn't know how to explain it to the rest of us. That's why we need you, sir.'

'Well, I don't think I can fix this without ruining the work that he's done. Can you bring him here?'

'No, sir. We don't know where he is today. He's like that. But we'll talk to him tonight and ask him to come tomorrow, sir.'

'That won't help. I'll be away for the next couple of weeks.'

There was a chorus of gasps, all dismayed.

'Where will you be, sir?'

'I'm going to India for a holiday with my brother.'

'But we finish on the eighteenth of June, sir. Today is the last day we'll see you.'

I nodded.

'Then you must come and have lunch with us.'

A whole year of teaching them, I thought, and they don't invite me to lunch until the last day. Was this another case where I'd missed all the invitations because I didn't recognise them?

'I saw sir in the movie,' said a student I couldn't place.

The whole class was sitting at the same long table in the student cafeteria. They'd all brought their own plates and cups from their rooms and they'd managed to scrounge a set for me too.

I swallowed down a mouthful of *ema datshi*, glad that they'd avoided giving me the dried fish but still disappointed at the quality of the college food.

'You saw *Druk Ge Goem?*'

The rest of the class looked at me with wide eyes.

'Was sir in *Druk Ge Goem?*'

'Does sir know Michael?'

It took most of the meal to divert them from questions about the movie star, but I eventually got to ask what they planned once they finished at RIM.

'It all depends on our final results,' said Deki. Of course I hope to stay in Thimphu, but I'll probably get placed in Samtse or somewhere.'

'Placed?' I asked. 'Don't you have to look for jobs?'

'No. We're already guaranteed a job in the government. We passed the exams two years ago. Now we just have to find out which town and which department we're going to work in.'

It explained so much about why they never seemed particularly interested in studying. The marks didn't make it easier for them to get a job. They just determined their initial assignments. If only I'd known that from the beginning, I wouldn't have tried so hard either.

I breathed a long sigh of relief as I stepped off the bus onto the familiar ground of Thimphu. My brother and I had spent more time together in the last two weeks than we had in the previous fifteen years and I'd enjoyed experiencing India with him. But sixteen hours on a crowded train and another eight on a bus had returned all the stress I'd managed to shed on the break. I'd given Dominique the space she'd said she needed, but as drained as I felt now, there'd be no smile to entice her to me when I got home. I hoisted my pack onto my back and began the trudge through town.

A young man, barely more than a boy, appeared at my side, matching my steps. I turned my head to see his wide grin. He gestured that I should run, taking a couple of steps ahead before turning back to me.

I shook my head. Not in the mood. Too tired.

He jogged back, grabbed my arm and pulled me along, laughing.

It was so out of place that I couldn't help but join the laughter. I allowed myself to be dragged up the street until my feet got tangled and I had to put on the brakes.

He turned again, smiling, gesturing and grunting and I realised he was deaf. Or playing deaf. Beggars carrying 'official' papers to proclaim their disabilities and requesting assistance had begun to turn up in Bhutan recently. They didn't seem to realise that begging was illegal here. Their papers were obviously forgeries.

My smile faded as I prepared myself to tell him that I didn't believe him. I certainly wouldn't give him any money.

He lifted his arm in the light bulb screwing gesture. Where are you going?

'Home,' I told him. I live here. I'm not a gullible tourist with lots of money to throw away.

His response was to give me the thumbs up, run on the spot, then, still grinning, take off across the street.

Once again my western suspicion had gotten the better of me. This boy was the embodiment of Gross National Happiness. The Bhutan I'd come to love in my first weeks was still here if I cared to look. I began to jog home, unconcerned by the heavy pack.

Dominique would be delighted by my smile, I thought as I opened the door to our flat. But she wasn't there. Instead, there was a note.

Gone east for a couple of weeks.
We need to talk when I get back.

The walk to the UN offices took me down the long hill, past the neighbourhood garbage pit. It wasn't the best road to be on while wearing a suit, but that couldn't be helped. I was running late and the suit might help me convince the UN to let a school use their video-conferencing equipment to join a multinational education program.

I still didn't know when Dominique would be back, but I'd taken her advice. It was proving tricky to find archers that used traditional bows, but at least I'd found an online group of Bhutanese writers. Some were interested in meeting face to face.

My thoughts were broken by wild barks and the scream of a child. I looked across the street to see a boy of about six surrounded by large angry strays. I'd never seen this pack mentality in daylight.

While I searched for a way across the busy street to help him, a part of me marvelled at his presence of mind. Had it been me, I'd probably have run away, exposing my back, or curled up in a ball. This boy had a stick in hand and was swinging it wildly at the dogs while screaming his fury. As long as his energy held out, they wouldn't get near him.

A man walking up my side of the street waved his arms and shouted '*sha!*' to no effect.

I'd just started to scream at the cars to stop and let us across when a taxi pulled up beside the boy and the driver rolled down his window. The repeated thud as he whacked his door sent the dogs scattering and the taxi drove away.

The boy continued his walk down the hill, unconcerned.

This late on a Tuesday evening, the Thimphu writing group had Centrepoint restaurant to ourselves. I had little idea what Wangdi could do to improve the romantic poem he'd chosen to read, but then, his eyes had betrayed his incomprehension too as I'd read my science fiction piece. The same was true for Ram. No matter, I gathered that both the Bhutanese just wanted an appreciative audience rather than real feedback they could use to better their writing.

'Beautiful, Wangdi,' I said. 'Is it about the same woman as the last piece?'

He picked up his beer and stared at it. 'Yes. She's studying in India and I miss her so much. I write these poems to try to get her to come home.'

'I wish I could write like that,' said Ram, who'd shared a similar piece of his own.

The group wasn't what I'd planned. I'd loved a book of Bhutanese fables by Tshering Tshering and a story about a stray dog by Kunzang Choden. It was unrealistic to expect that such accomplished writers would find their way to the group on its first gathering, but I'd hoped for some inspiration from other writers of prose. Never mind. Writing groups are built on all styles and levels and we'd get a diverse style base once we grew the membership.

'Murray, I have to apologise for what Pema Dorji said on the forum.' Ram picked up his own beer and took a swig while I savoured my whisky. 'All that stuff about foreigners being parasites – he's just bitter. We don't all think like that.'

I sat back, trying to exude calm. 'I know you don't, Ram. Enough people jumped on him for that comment, but he got some things right. We do have problems in Australia and perhaps I should be putting effort into finding a way to solve those rather than travelling the world.'

Wangdi sat up straighter. 'Are your problems as bad as in Bhutan?'

'Far worse, I'd say. Bhutan may not be perfect, but your people are generally well fed and the racial differences aren't crippling.'

'But for crime? Do little girls get raped?'

'I don't know the statistics,' I said, emptying my glass, 'but I believe it happens a lot.' I knew he was thinking of a recent case in Thimphu. 'One case doesn't make this a bad country.'

The wife of a soldier, living in the barracks area, had been trying to manage both her daughter and her washing when the phone rang. Her neighbour, a soldier friend of the husband, offered to take care of the girl and the woman had gratefully accepted. Half an hour later, he'd delivered her back, screaming. Unable to calm the girl down, the woman thought it might be a full nappy. Instead, she found enormous amounts of blood. A doctor confirmed that the girl had been raped. She was eleven months old.

'I hope he gets raped himself, now that he's in gaol.'

'That doesn't sound very Buddhist,' I said.

Wangdi stuffed his papers into his bag as the waitress cleared the table. 'There are limits even to Buddhism. I'm one of the lenient ones. Many people think this is worth the death penalty.'

I heard a scratching in the kitchen as soon as I walked through the door. 'Bloody rats.' Weren't they meant to avoid higher storeys?

'That's not very nice,' said Dominique, startling me. She appeared in the kitchen doorway, looking sheepish as she walked over to give me a hug. 'Where have you been?'

It took a few moments to find my voice, so I just held her. 'We had the first writing group tonight. I didn't know when you were coming back.'

'I wanted to surprise you.' She leaned up for a kiss. 'It's good to see you smiling again. I've missed it.' She took my hand and started towards the bedroom.

I briefly wondered what had happened to the promised talk, but the thought died quickly. I followed.

The doctor and I both sat on wooden school chairs in his office.

'What is the problem?' he asked.

I shrugged, embarrassed. 'My stomach's been bloated all night. I've been farting and burping until it's normal, but five minutes later it's bloated again.'

Dominique hadn't been too impressed to find me lying in my study when she got up. 'We finally find our way back to each other and you decide to sleep somewhere else!' she'd said. When I'd told her of my symptoms, she'd gone into panic. 'But Murray, that's giardia. You can die from that.'

And so I'd ended up agreeing to go to both the hospitals for a diagnosis for what amounted to a wind problem.

'I see. I'll need to take your pulse,' said the doctor of traditional medicine.

For the thirty seconds that he held my wrist, I worried that he would send me for acupuncture.

He spun around to his desk and scribbled a note. 'Take this to the counter.'

I waited in the sun, an old lady walking circles around a large prayer wheel beside me, while my prescription was made up. Half an hour later, I walked away with three bags of small herbal pellets and instructions to take one of each with every meal.

I still had no idea what the diagnosis was.

I was given a token at the Jigme Dorji National Referral Hospital and waited my turn to see the doctor. When I was eventually ushered into his office, I found three other patients already being examined. While one of his students attended to me, the doctor asked his patient to remove her top so he could examine her breasts, presumably for cancer. I turned away, though no one else seemed concerned about privacy.

'Lift your shirt, please.'

The student placed her hand on my stomach, which by now was acting normally. In even less time than the last doctor, she gave me a prescription.

'Drinking salts for dehydration and vitamin B for your appetite.'

Medicine for a hypochondriac.

'What's for dinner?'

Without turning around, I told Dominique it was chilli con carne.

She snorted. 'You're so predictable. Whatever it is smells good. Did you find some meat?'

'Yep. I wanted something special to welcome you home, but you distracted me last night.'

'So what are you making?'

'I told you.'

'Fine. Call me when it's ready, whatever it is. I've got lots of work to do.'

As soon as she left, I tipped a can of baked beans over the chillies and the meat that I'd spent two hours chopping into mince. Then I lightly boiled some carrot and broccoli and added those, served it all up with rice and called her to the table.

'Voilà. Chilli con carne.'

She looked up in shock. 'You really did it?' Her eyes were shining to match the smile that I'd missed for so long. I barely had time to sit down before she'd grabbed me into a hug, one I readily returned.

'Well, it's a poor effort, but the best my meagre skills could manage with the ingredients available.'

'It doesn't matter,' she said, taking a mouthful. 'It's delicious.'

We ate in silence for a while, as I savoured the sight of her.

'So what else happened while I was away?' she asked eventually.

I pulled out the latest newspaper. 'China's been busy. In the last week, they've completed the railway to Lhasa in Tibet and they've reopened the Silk Road into India.'

Her horror recalled mine when I'd first read the articles. 'What does that mean for Bhutan? It'll be so much easier for the Chinese engineers to finish the road into Bhutan and get their armies here.'

'I haven't seen any comments by Bhutanese officials, but I'd say you're right. They must be panicking.'

Silence again, bordering on uncomfortable. It had been so long since we'd really talked that conversation was still difficult. Dominique was the first to speak. 'They finally found someone to work on my database.'

'About bloody time.'

A cheeky grin flickered over her face and was gone. 'She's not sure she can do it. Apparently her teacher wasn't very good, but at least I now know why it took a year for the request to be filled.'

'Why? Which department has she come from?'

The grin returned. 'Her name's Deki Wangmo and she just graduated from RIM.'

It was one of the first sunny days we'd had in weeks. Or perhaps it was just the first one I'd noticed. When the sun shower began, I moved to the office window and watched the locals scurry for cover under shop awnings. A rainbow formed over the monastery at the end of the valley.

'Somebody died,' said Yeshey behind me.

'What? Who?' I asked before noticing he didn't look upset. Had I misheard him?

'It's what we believe when it rains while the sun's out.'

I couldn't resist. 'Someone's dying all the time, Yeshey. Do you mean someone you know? Or someone in Thimphu since everyone in Thimphu is having the same experience?'

He laughed. 'I don't know. It's just what we believe.'

The road to Haa led over Chele La, at four thousand metres the highest point of road in the country. We'd seen nothing but bitumen for most of the drive over and down the other side. When the mist finally cleared, I saw that Haa was a lush green valley and the town was busy with activity even on a Sunday.

Dominique had invited me to join her on a weekend research trip and the paperwork had gone through in time.

'Do you think it's some kind of festival?' I asked as we negotiated our way through the crowds. From the wave of stunned expressions in our wake, it was clear that Haa didn't see many *chilips*.

'I didn't hear about it, but then no one tells me much. Oh, there he is.'

We stopped so Dominique could run out and grab a young man who was walking to join the crowd. I knew he must be Dominique's contact, the livestock agent in Haa.

'I'm so glad you came today,' he said once we'd been introduced. 'Now I don't have to join the clean-up.'

'What are you cleaning up?' I asked.

'The rivers mostly, but the area around the town in general. People still don't realise that the plastic stays forever, so every year we get the whole town together to clean it up. We hope that they'll get so sick of it that they'll manage their own garbage properly.'

'How would they do that?' asked Dominique. 'If they use plastic, where will they put it?'

'We have trucks that take it all to India. They sort and recycle all the garbage down there.'

Dominique appeared back in the flat only minutes after she left.

'Forget something?' I called from the study.

I heard her burst into tears and went to find her reaching for the phone. 'What's wrong?' I reached out a comforting hand, but she shrugged it away and slammed the phone back into the cradle.

When the tears had subsided, she said, 'I parked the car on the street last night and now the petrol's all gone.'

I didn't see the connection. 'Dominique, we did use a lot of petrol on the trip to Haa, but surely there's enough to get to the station to fill it up.'

Fury replaced the tears. 'I'm not dumb. I filled it up yesterday and now it's gone. Take a look yourself if you don't believe me. They cut the hose and they siphoned out the fuel. It's very common now, apparently.' She collapsed onto the sofa bench. 'Why does this always happen to me? It must be *karma*, but what have I done to deserve this?'

I sat down next to her, but far enough away not to warrant the rejection again. Let her come to me. 'One problem isn't *karma*, Dominique. You can take a taxi to work. I'll get the car fixed today.'

'You don't get it, do you? It's not just the car. They're not going to renew my contract.'

Dominique wasn't there when I looked back. We were well matched cycling on the flats and the road to the end of the Thimphu valley was long rather than steep so she should have been right behind me. I found her around the previous bend, trying to pump up her tyre and muttering about *karma* again.

I ran my hand around the wheel until I found a nail that had gone right through the tube and jammed into the rim. 'You won't be able to pump this up.'

'Why does it always happen to me?'

I put out my hand to touch her, but drew back. Let her come to me. 'It was bound to happen eventually, Dominique. We've been riding for almost a year without a puncture kit. I'm amazed it's taken this long. It's not such a big deal.'

'That's easy for you to say. You're not the one who has to push their bike twenty kilometres to get home. And you don't have a report to finish before the end of the year.'

'That's not fair, Dominique. I'm busy too and I need to get a real project under my belt so I don't have to start from scratch when we move to Mongolia or wherever next.'

'You can't wait to move, can you? This is great for you. You always say that I'm the only reason you're here.'

'That's not what I mean, Dominique, and you know it. Now let's get this sorted out. Wasn't that a taxi parked outside the house a few corners back?'

I was right and the taxi driver was out the front when we arrived. He moved with purpose, carrying firewood.

'Can you give Dominique a lift back to town? She got a flat tyre.'

The driver gave the bike a quick glance before apologising. 'Sorry. I'm busy. I've got visitors coming.'

Fair enough. We'd have to walk.

'The monks are coming for a *puja*,' he said as he walked away.

'Surely helping someone in need would be better for your *karma* than performing a ritual,' I called after him, but he was already inside.

'Shall we go?' I asked Dominique as the credits rolled on the DVD. It was Saturday evening and our friends' party would have started already.

'Before we go, Murray, I have to tell you something.'

'Sure.' Dominique had been finding more time for me over the past few weeks. I was convinced things were finally improving.

'Remember I left that note saying that we needed to talk? Well, I've been thinking a lot lately, about us, about what we're going to do next year.' She drew in a deep breath and held it for a second. 'Murray, I think it's only fair to tell you that if you asked me to move to Australia, I wouldn't go.'

Was that all? I took her hand. 'I'm not asking you to move to Australia. I just need you to consider me when you choose your next assignment.

Just choose a place that has internet access, so I can keep working on my company.'

'No. I can't do that. I need to go wherever is best for my career.'

'So, you're going to accept the job in Nepal?'

'I don't know. But I thought you should know how I feel.'

'Does that mean that you want me to stop working on the company?'

'No. I don't want you to come at all. You could work in Singapore. You said there's a lot of IT work there.'

I sat, stunned. I'd told her again and again that a distance marriage was not a relationship as far as I was concerned.

'Why, Dominique? You know that I've always supported your career.'

'Because of that. Because you've always been there when I've needed support and I need to know that I can do this on my own.'

'But you don't need to do it on your own. We vowed to be together.' At least I thought I did. I never did bother to find out exactly what I said yes to.

'I'm sorry.' She rubbed her feet together. 'What are you going to do?'

I wiped away a tear that stuck on my lip. 'If it wasn't for everything else I'm working on, I'd book a plane for tomorrow. But I'm still hoping to get a project with one of the development agencies.'

It was a struggle to control my voice. 'There's also a project I've been working on to get a Bhutanese class connected to schools in the US by video-conference. And I've just got the writing group going. It'll fall over if I leave.' I gathered up my courage. 'I guess we should just enjoy the time we have left and I'll plan to leave at the end of February when my visa runs out.'

She nodded, sadly. 'I'm going to the party now. Will you come?'

'I don't think so.'

I sat in the Centrepoint restaurant, not tasting the food I swallowed, idly turning pages of the Kuensel newspaper. Dominique filled my head. I'd stay for all the reasons I said, but I'd also stay in case she came to her senses. Once I'd gone to the effort of moving back to Australia, there would be no point in trying again. If it couldn't work here and now, it couldn't work.

An article caught my eye, distracting me even from my failed relationship.

A hailstorm had destroyed more than ten acres of corn crops and damaged chilli plantations in a town in the east of Bhutan last week. Kuensel reported that locals believed someone probably visited a forbidden lake nearby. A local resident told the journalist: 'If somebody has visited the lake, they are solely responsible for the misfortune.'

As silly as it sounded, I thought, there might be a shred of fact in there. If it was possible that a butterfly in Brazil could cause a typhoon in China, then why wasn't it possible for movement near a lake to cause a hailstorm locally? But I still wondered how this fit Buddhist beliefs. Surely everyone affected had their own karmic debt to pay and was personally responsible.

How seriously could Bhutanese people be taking their religion if they wouldn't help people in need and blamed everyone else for their problems? It seemed to me that Buddhism had become just another religion, full of ritual, a way for people to avoid responsibility for their own misfortune and even used as a tool to manipulate its followers.

I was already eating when Dominique came home.

'Is there any left for me?' she asked, sitting close beside me.

I put my arm around her. She'd relaxed further since she'd told me her plans. Since I'd given her up. 'Not much. I thought you were going to *taikwondo* tonight.'

'I was, but I had to go to the hospital with Deki Wangmo.'

'Is she okay?'

'Yes. I mean, I don't know. We went to see her brother. He was beaten with a cricket bat or something last night. Deki didn't recognise him because his face was all caved in.'

I stiffened. Not this. Was it only because everyone knew each other here that we heard about brutal crimes more often than anywhere else I'd lived? Was it because of the racial tension with the Southern Bhutanese? Or was it because of the violence on TV? Was Bhutan going the way of Nepal?

'Where did it happen?' I asked.

It was a while before Dominique answered, her voice quiet when she did. 'He was found just outside Seasons. He couldn't have moved by himself, so unless they dumped him there, it probably happened right in the middle of town.'

There was nothing to say. We both walked that path every day and often at night. So I just held her.

I felt her tear on my cheek as she whispered the last words. 'There were six people like that in the critical ward.'

High above Thimphu, a yak herder's hut stood overlooking the Dagala valley like the inspiration for Jim Craig's hut. The yak herder and his beautiful daughter waved us on our way to the Dagala Lakes, smiles broad from the honour of having their photo taken. Michael and I had decided to take the trek while our wives were busy working.

'Don't be surprised if you find my sleeping bag empty during the night,' said our guide, Hodor, turning to wave.

Norbu, the forestry official who'd joined us, shot back, 'As if she'd let you into her bed.'

'You obviously didn't see how she was looking at me.'

'I thought you trained as a monk,' I teased.

'Why do you think I quit?'

'Would you really walk all the way back?' asked Michael. 'You said our campsite is still a couple of hours away.'

'For a night between those legs, looking into those eyes? Perhaps I should go back now.' He pointed ahead. 'You can just follow this track to the end of the valley and turn left to find the campsite.' He started back the way we'd come.

Laughing, I grabbed his shoulders and swung him back around. 'Oh no you don't.'

Hodor slapped my hands away. 'You're no fun.'

'Is that how it really works, Norbu?' I asked. 'Is night hunting really about climbing into the window of a girl you've only spoken a few words to? Not that there were any windows in their hut.'

'No. He's dreaming.'

Hodor grinned. 'Honestly, I'd be extremely lucky to be invited in tonight. Girls like to be wooed. If I come up here for a night every few weeks and sit outside her hut, singing of her beauty or telling her of the life we could have together, she might let me in after a couple of months.'

We walked along lost in our own thoughts for another kilometre.

'It'd be worth it though, wouldn't it?' said Hodor. 'Did you see those eyes? You can keep your sleeping bags tonight, boys. I'm going hunting.'

Mist drifted across the lake, obscuring and revealing myriad shades of red and yellow moss covering the rocks around its edge.

'Keep your voices down around these lakes,' said Hodor. 'The goddess in these parts doesn't like noise and will bring in a mist so thick we'll never find our way out again.'

'Hodor, how can you abide superstition like that? I thought Buddhism was meant to be more philosophy than religion.'

Hodor's expression was stern. 'Our local gods belong to old beliefs from before Buddhism came to Bhutan, and they're an important part of the culture we're trying hard to keep. But Buddhism doesn't deny gods of any religion.'

We kept talking as we climbed higher into the cold mist. A network of hundreds of ponds were linked by walls of multi-hued moss.

'So how do *puja* and all the rituals help? How can a ceremony improve your *karma*? It doesn't make any sense to me.'

'It doesn't really make any sense to most Bhutanese either, but that's the point. It doesn't really matter what you do if it achieves the right result. A lot of Buddhism is intellectual, trying to control our behaviour and helping people understand the path to enlightenment. But there's another side that links directly into the subconscious.'

He stepped around a craggy rock and looked up for a way through to the next lake.

'Monks and scholars do all the thinking, but everyone can do the rituals, even when they don't understand the significance. You don't need to understand meditation to benefit from it.'

He seemed to find the path he was looking for and pressed on.

'Routines are a form of meditation, helping people delve into their subconscious. Even superstition is good when it keeps people from rushing off in new directions without thinking.'

'Like rushing to spend the night with a beautiful girl?'

'Touché.'

My hand found a flat stone while I pondered his words. I tried to skim it over the flat surface of the lake, but it flipped on the second bounce and dived under the surface with a plop.

'Now you've done it. Come on. Let's get back before the mists can trap us. In fact, I think we'd better start walking out before lunch.'

'Are you sure we came this way?'

Michael, a metre away, was just visible through the mist. 'No, but Hodor said to keep following the track.'

Hodor, Norbu and the horseman had stayed to tie the packs to the horses, but they should only have been ten minutes behind us. It had been over an hour since we left the camp.

Michael looked back the way we'd come. 'With all this mist, it'd be easy to get turned around.'

'But there's only one valley,' I said. 'As long as we walk downhill, we can't go too far wrong. And when there's a right turn, we take that.'

'What if we missed it already? We should go back and look for them.'

'You're not thinking it's the goddess, are you, just because I skimmed a stone in the lake?'

Michael's silence left me less than certain as I followed him back up the track and I found myself jumping at every cold finger of air on the back of my neck.

'What was that?'

'Shhh.' I'd heard something too. An eerie wail.

It came again. A voice in the mist on the opposite side of the valley. A Bhutanese cooee. 'Aaaaue!'

We called back and heard it again, louder now as though the caller had turned to face us.

'Great. At least we've found the right valley this time.'

We'd backtracked almost to the camp before we found a path up the side of the valley into a new one. Fresh hoofprints suggested we'd got it right this time, but the mist could make anyone nervous.

'Where have you been?' asked Hodor when we reached the end of the valley. 'I was worried you'd gotten properly lost.'

We explained the mistake as we moved on to the now-empty yak hut where Norbu and the horseman waited. I knew that winter was closing in and the herders would be moving to lower ground.

'It seems Hodor scared them off last night,' said Norbu, apparently unconcerned by our adventure.

'Come on. It's too late to make it all the way back today, but we should at least be able to get below the mist before we camp.'

I met Pema at a drinks session thrown by the honorary consul of Bhutan to Australia, when she visited late in the year. Pema had a senior position at RENEW, the organisation that looked after women's interests.

'Helping poor and disadvantaged women might be what we do mostly now, but it all started because of night hunting,' she told me.

'I thought night hunting was harmless,' I said.

She frowned at me over her glass. 'It is harmless for men.'

Here we go, I thought. It was time for the feminist rant. But Pema had probably never heard of bra burning. She was clearly an intelligent, caring woman who was doing her best to maintain a place for women in a world rapidly being taken over by men.

'You know that RENEW was started by one of the queens, Ashi Sangay Choden Wangchuck, right? Well, when she was touring the country, she was approached by many women complaining about night hunting not being consensual. It was rape. The women had little say in what happened and then got burdened with the baby.'

It was the first time I'd heard the dark side of the story, but I could see no reason to doubt her. 'So what is RENEW doing about it?'

'Night hunting may soon become illegal.'

'That seems harsh. I understand that you can't tolerate rape, but it would be sad to throw away a custom that's so unique to Bhutan and brings many people pleasure.' I clearly wasn't convincing her, but I pushed on. 'Isn't Bhutan trying to create a unique culture so India and China can't claim that you're culturally descended from them? Why create new customs when you have such fascinating customs already?'

'That's a very male perspective. It may be true that we're cultivating cultural distinction, but it can't be done at the expense of the happiness of our people.'

'Surely it's not always rape.'

She gave me that frown again. 'How many women have you heard talking about the pleasures of night hunting? It's our shame.'

I couldn't think of any, but then Pema was the first Bhutanese woman who'd been ready to talk about such things with me.

She sighed. 'You're right. It's not black and white. It doesn't have to be bad, but how do we tell the good cases from rape? It's simpler to ban it entirely.'

'Isn't that how couples form here?' I asked, thinking the implications through. 'You'd need to adopt a whole new way of dating.'

'The kids in the nightclubs don't seem to have any trouble with that idea.'

I stopped in front of the policeman guarding the entrance to Paro Dzong.

Raj, one of Yeshey's staff, walked on a few paces before realising I wasn't following and turned around. 'What are you doing?'

'All *chilips* have to sign in here,' I said.

'Not today, you don't. You're here on official business.'

The policeman made no move to stop me and I felt a thrill at being an insider at last.

Raj led the way up ancient wooden steps to an open defensive platform. From there it was a short step down a corridor to the server room where plywood and flashing lights ruined the atmosphere of the 350-year-old castle. It was also the first computer room I'd ever seen that was open to the outside air. Beyond the shutters was the balcony and anyone who happened to pass by.

'Can you help Tshering Dorji with his computer?' asked Raj once he'd shown me the design of the network.

I followed his directions down dark corridors of wood. The floorboards I walked on were smooth from centuries of monks' footsteps. The walls carried the echoes of robes rustling through history.

Tshering Dorji's room was small, the compressed-mud walls more than a metre thick, but the bright yellow paint gave a feeling of space. As I installed a virus scanner on his computer, I wondered if those walls had ever needed repairing. Were these floorboards and walls still from the original structure?

'Just think,' I said in awe. 'This room has probably been a monk's room for the last few hundred years.'

'Not a monk. A warrior's, I think.'

'Either way, how does it feel to work in a room with that much history?'

He thought for a while. 'The history's okay. It's the smell of urine that bothers me.'

'What a nice bunch of blokes,' I said to Raj on the drive home. I was on a high from my first day of working in a real castle.

'They are,' he said, before adding nervously, 'but sir, please don't tell Yeshey about lunch.'

'Sure.' The fact that the Paro officers had shouted us lunch in the store just outside the castle didn't seem worth mentioning to me. 'But why not?'

'Because he gave me money for lunch and if you tell him that we didn't pay, I'll have to give it back. I don't get much money as it is, so I rely on the daily allowance.'

I remembered Yeshey's semi-serious claims that Southern Bhutanese weren't to be trusted and wondered just how much Raj had saved this way. The cost of one meal wouldn't go far. I was debating whether to say something to him when we rounded a corner and saw a truck hanging over the embankment, its rear wheels clinging to the verge.

We both jumped out as soon as I'd stopped the car, shouting as we ran to help.

A couple of young men appeared from around the far side, apparently unharmed. They didn't speak English so I let Raj make sure that they were okay while I inspected the site. It didn't take a forensic expert to put together the basics, but Raj confirmed it for me.

'They're a bit shaken up, but otherwise okay. It seems they swerved to the side to avoid a crazy taxi that came round the corner too fast.'

I pointed to the ground between the two back wheels. 'Then the untarred road gave way.' I'd often sworn at truck drivers for keeping their large, well-treaded tyres on the tar and forcing me to drive our little car right to the verge. Now I understood that the roadside would hold the car's weight but not the truck's.

'Yes. The truck started to go over and he turned down the hill for some reason.'

I looked down to the valley a couple of hundred metres below. 'If he hadn't, he probably would have rolled the truck all the way to the bottom and they'd both be dead. But what courage would it take to actually steer the truck over the edge?'

'And what good *karma* to hit the only tree in sight?'

Michael joined me for lunch at Centrepoint and I told him about the truck accident of the day before.

'Those bloody taxis are going to cause a real problem one day,' said Michael.

'You can't generalise about taxis like that,' I said, thinking that we did the same thing in Australia.

Michael took a mouthful of his rice omelette. 'Maybe not, but remember what Mick said when he was testing taxi drivers?'

I shook my head. It had been a long time since I'd thought about the man who'd been sent home.

'He said that whenever he failed them, they gave him a sob story about having to feed their families and that his colleagues urged him to reconsider. Who knows how many got licences without actually passing their tests.'

The waitress brought my ginger pork and I sent her back for chopsticks. Unlike some of the patrons, she'd known Michael before his fame and didn't stare.

'Did you hear about the new driving test they're going to bring in?' I asked.

'Yeah. They called it rigorous in the paper, but it's just a written test. I doubt it will make much of a difference.'

'I do. It should at least reduce the number of people driving down the wrong side of the road and people who push out into roundabouts when there's traffic already on them.'

Michael shook his head. 'Even the police don't seem to know the rules. They stand at the roundabouts all day, but only jump in once a gridlock occurs.'

A thought came to me. 'Perhaps they don't have the same rules. We automatically think that because they use international road devices and markings that they use international rules, but what if they have their own?'

We both looked out the window at the road below, trying to make sense of the chaos.

'No,' Michael said finally. 'It's the law of the jungle. The bigger beast wins.'

I came out of the shop to find a four-wheel-drive parked in the driveway. Michael's words of the previous week came back to me.

Adrenaline rushed through my body, readying me for a fight. Why should I let some big beast make me wait? The driveway was wide enough that I could have driven our small car past it if he'd parked to the side. An extra few seconds would have been enough for the owner to drive into the car park properly. I stormed back into the store and growled, 'Whose truck is that?'

A young man standing in line at the counter looked up. 'That's mine,' he said proudly.

'You've parked me in.' I spoke as if to a half-wit, wondering if he was. I pointed at my car just in case he hadn't noticed it.

He looked unconcerned. 'I was only going to be a couple of minutes.'

'So was I, but I didn't park someone else in.'

'How was I meant to know that was your car?'

Words almost failed me, but I managed a final coherent sentence before anger took over. 'It doesn't matter whose car it is. Parked in. Move.'

'You could be polite about it,' he said, still not moving.

I should have said, 'Is it polite to park the way you did? Is it Buddhist?' Instead, all I could manage was a glare while I waited for him to pay.

Behind the glass screen of the learner's permit counter, the woman in charge looked at me blankly. 'What licence do you have?'

'What?' I asked, showing her my licence. 'Do the road rules depend on what licence you have?'

'Yes, that's fine,' she said. 'I don't see the problem.'

I shook my head, trying to clear the nonsense. 'The problem is that I've never seen official rules for driving in Bhutan. You know, like exactly what the signs mean.'

The young man beside me, who'd been trying to get the woman's attention, joined the conversation. 'We get a book like this to study when we get our licence. Is it what you're looking for?'

I took the book he was holding out and flicked through it. Aside from the contact details and signatures, there were a couple of pages of street signs. I pointed to one.

'I've never seen this here. It just tells you that there's a roundabout coming up. How do you tell who has right of way?'

His stare matched the counter woman's.

I tried again. 'At a roundabout, do you give way to the right or the left?'

'It depends on which roundabout.'

I woke up at five, realising that Dominique hadn't slept in our bed. She was on the spare mattress in my study and woke as I entered. Without a word, she got up and went to shower. I started up my laptop and waited for her to finish.

She was about to go away again for another couple of weeks. I'd hoped to spend a bit of time with her before she left, but all weekend she'd run away every time I saw her, choosing to eat with friends and work elsewhere. Last night, she'd packed her bags around me, but apparently couldn't sleep in the same room.

I allowed her a little time to dress after the shower stopped, then went in and leaned on the door frame.

Finally, she turned to me. 'When I come back, I'll find somewhere else to stay.'

There was little left in me to hurt. 'Don't bother. I won't be here when you come back. My business is meaningless if we're not together and the rest just isn't worth it.'

With tears in her eyes, Dominique gave me a hug and kissed my neck, then picked up her bags and walked out.

I had two weeks to find a flight home.

The accident happened the day before I left. I was taking my bike down to be boxed up for shipping and drove through the southern traffic circle where one policeman directed traffic and another one or two stood around ready to educate drivers who did the wrong thing. Just five metres down the hill from the circle was a pedestrian crossing and an Indian man was making his way over. Anybody else would have rushed through, perhaps giving him the horn as they did. That had become habit for me too, but today it occurred to me that there was no other reason for marking a zebra crossing except to give pedestrians a safe place to cross. I decided it was time to set things right. Already going slow after manoeuvring around the circle, I braked to a stop. The jolt of impact occurred just as the pedestrian waved thanks. In my rear view mirror I saw a motorbike helmet disappearing to one side.

By the time I got out of the car, a policeman was already there, seeing to the two people on the bike. One looked very groggy. I waited while the policeman spoke to them in Dzongkha, then in a gap I asked if the bloke was alright. The policeman turned, told me he was fine and made a brusque gesture of dismissal.

I drove to the end of the road and stopped out of sight before slumping my head on the wheel. Those men didn't deserve to be hurt. No one in this country did, but I'd caused them harm. By not following the local

customs, I'd done as much damage as if I'd hit the pedestrian. Both the
pedestrian and the driver of the bike, as well as many passers-by, would
be confused at crossings now. They wouldn't know what to expect from
anyone. It might cause more accidents.

Change has to come from within. The people had faith in their king to
lead them to a better future while maintaining their independence. He'd
determined, with their support, that this path required their culture to
be unique. If that caused its own problems, if that meant some concerns
went unaddressed for a while, that was their choice. They'd keep correcting
their course until they survived or failed. Why should I, who had grown
up with modern technology and what we call a higher standard of living,
think that I could tell them how to do this? For all their problems, they
were doing well on their own.

The customs official gave me a friendly smile as she stamped my passport,
seemingly unaware of the duty such people have to scowl. 'I hope you
enjoyed your stay, sir.'

I gave her a sad smile in return and walked through the waiting lounge
and on into the open air. The plane that would take me to Bangkok sat
on the tarmac in still silence. With only a couple of flights each day, the
airport staff were rarely overworked. My plane would already be serviced,
fuelled and ready to go. I breathed a sigh of relief. By this same early hour
the next day, I'd be with friends in Sydney.

An official waved me to one side. 'Please identify your luggage.'

I pointed out my black suitcase and green rucksack, thinking that it
was only a small part of the baggage I'd be taking with me into the future.
I'd gambled everything on a life with Dominique. We'd created a picture
of a life living cheaply in developing countries, helping where we could.

She'd work in agriculture and I'd do IT consulting and write about our experiences. With a bit of saving, we could buy a farmhouse in France to rent out, while we used the renovated barn as a base for home visits.

That dream was shattered and I felt empty, but I knew I'd recover. I just needed time. Perhaps I could even rebuild the dream as I rebuilt my life. I could set up a base in Sydney and rent it out to pay for my travels. There was a world full of interesting places out there that needed IT skills. One day I'd be ready to explore again, meeting people and learning from them. The idea of starting with the indigenous population from Australia appealed to me.

I'd collect more baggage along the way, but I knew I wouldn't regret any of it, just as I didn't regret the past two years. My time with Dominique had been troubled by misunderstandings and the pressure of an early marriage, but we'd had some great times. I still loved and admired her more than anyone else and she'd given me an experience few people have.

Tourists who came to Bhutan for a few weeks saw the Shangri-La image, but that was all. I'd seen deeper. I'd seen a country troubled by the pressures of its location, the political situation of the region and the world it was trying to join. It was a country plagued by the same kinds of issues that every other country has, no matter its political or economic circumstances. How could it not be? It was populated by humans.

Bhutan was also a country with its own unique take on the world and had taught me some significant lessons, even if I'd been slow to learn them. Happiness, I now knew, was a more worthwhile goal than financial gain. The best path to happiness was in making time for people, not in collecting expensive possessions. I still believed in science, but what I called superstition was growing on me as a valid model for explaining the world and left room for a touch of mystery. In the years ahead, until

I could rebuild my dream, I would have to work hard not to lose these wisdoms to the drone of life in the city.

I walked back inside the building and sat down to wait for the flight into my future. A Bhutanese man passed through the room and out to the tarmac to check his bags. His red, maroon and black *gho* was the same pattern as the one I'd fumbled with for months at the beginning of my stay. When he returned, he took a quick look around then came to sit across from me. He introduced himself and asked what I thought of Bhutan.

It was a question I knew the answer to by heart. 'It's a beautiful country and the people are very friendly,' I said.

But it was so much more than that.

ABOUT THE AUTHOR

Murray Gunn grew up in Sydney with parents who loved meeting people from different cultures. With an endless stream of international guests invited to stay in his home, each with their own story, it was inevitable that he would develop a passion for travel and experiencing different ways of life. After a decade of living and working overseas, he is currently back in Sydney studying anthropology and planning his next adventure.

The author has a strong belief in the need for Bhutan to determine its own direction as it finds its place in the future. Organisations like RENEW, Tarayana Foundation and VAST were founded by Bhutanese to address various problems as seen by the people themselves. Fifty per cent of the royalties from each book sold will go to support these and similar organisations working for the betterment of Bhutan.